Stella

Stella

UNREPENTANT MADAM

Linda J. Eversole

VICTORIA · VANCOUVER · CALGARY

TouchWood Editions
#108 – 17665 66A Avenue
Surrey, BC V3S 2A7
www.touchwoodeditions.com

LIBRARY AND ARCHIVES CANADA CATALOGUING IN PUBLICATION
Eversole, Linda J., 1950–
    Stella: unrepentant madam / Linda J. Eversole.

Includes bibliographical references and index.
ISBN 1-894898-31-1

    I. Carroll, Stella.   2. Prostitutes—British Columbia—Victoria—Biography.
3. Prostitutes—United States—Biography.   4. Prostitution—British Columbia—
Victoria—History—20th century.   I. Title.

HQ142.E94 2005   306.74'092   C2005-904992-8

Edited by Marlyn Horsdal
Book design and layout by Jacqui Thomas
Cover photo from the John Carroll collection

Printed in Canada

TouchWood Editions acknowledges the financial support for its publishing program
from the Government of Canada through the Book Publishing Industry
Development Program (BPIDP), Canada Council for the Arts, and the British
Columbia Arts Council.

THIS BOOK HAS BEEN PRODUCED ON 100% POST-CONSUMER RECYCLED PAPER,
PROCESSED CHLORINE FREE AND PRINTED WITH VEGETABLE-BASED DYES.

For My Mother
Helen Menzies (Eversole) Porter

1914–2001

Contents

Acknowledgments

I am at a loss as to how to thank all the people who assisted and supported me in unravelling the complex life of Stella Carroll. Having spent in excess of 20 years tracking Stella from Missouri to California and British Columbia and back, I have been in touch with countless archives, museums and government offices, and their knowledgeable staff. There are far too many people to thank individually without running the risk of glaring oversights, but I am grateful to those who have shown interest and on several occasions have brought to my attention material that I might have missed.

To my colleagues in the heritage world in both Canada and the United States, whose work is often undervalued: so much would be lost without your dedication in preserving our history. We may not be able to see into the future, but we can use our past, as long as we are willing to learn from it, to guide us forward. That is because you care.

To the Carroll family—Roy, Dorothy, John and Mary Rood—your honesty, loyalty, warmth, and humour helped me to know Stella in much more personal way. I am greatly appreciative of your generosity in sharing your photographs and memories of her. This book couldn't have been written without you. Also thanks to the late Cecil Temple and Katherine Lewis, both of whom showed me the Stella they knew.

To my own family and very good friends whose love, interest and encouragement always spurred me on—especially Christopher, Machala, Cheryl, Greg, Kathleen, Gerry, Vera, Frank and of course my mom, Helen. Thanks always.

I am indebted to my editor Marlyn Horsdal, who, with her meticulous editing and constructive suggestions, helped me to bring Stella to life.

And to Stella, whose unseen ghost has travelled with me for many years. I bet you are as surprised and relieved as I am that this is finally finished!

Linda J. Eversole

one

What the Duce [sic] Can Be the Matter,
For in my Heart There's Such a Clatter[1]

*S*TELLA CARROLL CAREFULLY sorted through her jewellery, searching for just the right piece to wear. She enjoyed inspecting her impressive and strikingly large diamonds. They glittered and sparkled but they also represented her investments, her security and her achievements. She loved to adorn herself with them and now decided to fix her particular favourite, a starburst diamond brooch, in her lustrous auburn hair. Its beauty would be lost against the ivory colour of her dress but would stand out in her elaborate coiffure. As she readied herself for the late-night hours that her business demanded, she took a final glance in the mirror. This was her finest brothel and her image as madam set the tone. Her dress was handmade lace from Ireland and fit her buxom form beautifully. The undergarments

Stella in 1908. She was proud of her Irish heritage and had this lace dress made on one of her trips to Ireland. It suited her role as madam of Rockwood, her high-class parlour house in Victoria, B.C. [PRIVATE COLLECTION]

that created her shape were painfully restrictive but helped to keep her posture straight and stately, commanding good behaviour and exuding class. This was no downtown two-dollar house: that was made abundantly clear by the mere fact of her regal presence.

She had spent countless hours redecorating Rockwood. Her fastidious attention to detail had fashioned public rooms, such as her two parlours, that rivalled and indeed surpassed any of the better houses in town. Everything was top quality and spotless. Oriental rugs graced the floors, topped with soft leather armchairs for the men and low upholstered stools and small chairs for her girls. She had her new cylinder phonograph and the piano for entertainment and on each polished wood surface there was an arrangement of fresh flowers. The windows were shaded with velvet drapes and inner hangings of lace-trimmed sheers. The books and statuary she had bought on her trip to Europe were placed strategically around the main parlour. The leather and wood gave a masculine "private club" air to the room while the flowers and lace spoke to the enticing promise of the females who were the main attraction.

Stella glowed with pride as she wandered into one of the parlours, her five little dogs trotting along behind the train of her dress. It was at times like this that memories of the sod house would arise—the earth that constantly trickled down the walls, the muddy puddles on the floor after a rain, the dark. She shuddered: never again.

Her private quarters consisted of a sitting room and bedroom tastefully fitted out with a large ornate brass bed, chevalier mirror, wardrobe, dressing table and chintz-covered loveseat.

Stella loved animals: they were her surrogate children. She even had a portrait done of her five little dogs at Rockwood. [PRIVATE COLLECTION]

The girls' rooms were furnished with simpler brass beds, a dressing table, washstand and top-quality linens and carpets.

The practical "essentials" were placed discreetly out of sight. Condoms were available but not commonly used. They were not considered to be very effective for, as one physician put it, "at any moment it is liable to rupture and place the wearer in the position of the virtuous swain, who used an eel skin as a prophylactic and neglected to sew up the eye-holes."[2] Baskets with a selection of liquor and clean towels were ready to be delivered to each room when ordered by the client and everything was carefully positioned to show that this was the top parlour house in the city.

Stella Carroll was essentially a businesswoman: shrewd, clear-headed (except when it came to love) and experienced enough to know there would always be tough times for her high-risk trade. Yet it seemed that her recent difficulties were behind her, and in fact she was certain that 1911 could prove to be her best year so far. True, there were many who thought she was finished, particularly since her "accident," but she would show them all she would not be forced out. She must hold steady to her course and in time everything would settle down.

With Rockwood, on the outskirts of Victoria, she had finally achieved her goal of a luxurious, high-class operation that attracted the elite of the city. She was well on her way to

Stella inspects her new cylinder phonograph in her bedroom at Rockwood. She was fond of all kinds of music. [PRIVATE COLLECTION]

achieving the status held by Tessie Wall and Jessie Hayman in San Francisco. Despite setbacks, not the least of which was having her left leg amputated, she now owned two successful brothels—the other, on Herald Street, was downtown—several pieces of real estate and, of course, her diamonds.

Stella's business acumen had served her well when she chose this particular house for her country establishment. As with most real estate, its value was in the location, and for a brothel to appeal to a certain type of clientele it needed attributes other than the obvious ones of beautiful women, good food and liquor. Chief among these was easy and discreet accessibility. Although Rockwood was away from the centre of the city, it was well sited for a number of reasons, the most important being its proximity to the waterway known as "The Gorge" and the newly developed park that followed its shoreline. There was a decent road for cars and carriages, the park had a tramway system, and canoes could be rented to paddle up the winding channel.

This house was special to her, not only as her upscale brothel—or, as she preferred to think of it, parlour house—but also as her home.[3] It was large and spacious, befitting its original purpose as a family home. Designed by a prominent Victoria architect, John Teague, it was well built and the equal of the other grand houses nearby. The area, once home to a few small farms, had recently developed as a desirable residential neighbourhood and several of the city's wealthy citizens were buying up land for their country estates. Rockwood was one of the finest. It sat prominently on a hill and its tower could be seen from the other side of The Gorge. At the back

Stella loved fine jewellery. Here, she shows off her diamond rings, which she considered beautiful and a good investment. [PRIVATE COLLECTION]

of the house a long walkway of sapling-lined steps, with a railing on either side, descended through the garden to the private dock, providing an inconspicuous entrance for anyone arriving by water.

Stella was naïve, however, to have thought that the neighbours would welcome or even tolerate her, particularly as they included the current premier, Richard McBride. It was not as if they had to watch men going in and out; the house was well away from the road, down a long private drive. People just did not like her there, flaunting her activities on their very doorsteps, despite the fact that some of them were actually profiting from her presence. Premier McBride and his

The bridge in the Gorge area of Victoria, B.C., a neighbourhood that boasted expensive homes and a large recreational park. Neighbours were not happy to have Stella and her brothel in their midst. [PRIVATE COLLECTION]

The exterior of the front of Stella's Rockwood. [PRIVATE COLLECTION]

Conservative Party used Stella and her profession as a tool to discredit their political foes by exposing her private meetings and special operating arrangements with government officials. James "Tod" Aikman, the Saanich prosecutor, had profited many times from his participation in Stella's numerous court appearances and Thompson Kirby, a clerk at the Merchant's Bank who lived at 136 Gorge Road, had held a mortgage on Stella's Herald Street properties since 1909. There was nothing wrong with making money from a well-run, albeit morally questionable business, as long as it was in someone else's neighbourhood.

Friday was always a good night for business and this one was no exception. It was a typical August evening: the temperature

A set of stairs leading to a private dock allowed Stella's Rockwood visitors to arrive and depart by boat, which was convenient and discreet. [PRIVATE COLLECTION]

was beginning to cool and a slight breeze made it especially pleasant. Over on the waterfront a lull descended as families and young people packed up their summer picnics and returned home. The evening would bring a more adult crowd for the music of The Gorge orchestra and mezzo-soprano Madame Marie Burnett. There was also the outdoor theatre where motion pictures, such as tonight's features, *A Medium Wanted for a Son-In-Law* and *The Bride of the Gamekeeper*, would attract a crowd.

It was still fairly quiet at Stella's, as many of the local lads were watching the Pacific Coast League baseball match: the Victoria Islanders against the Tacoma Tigers. The Islanders led by two points until the seventh inning when, as a local sports correspondent put it, the Tigers "pounced." Two home runs in quick succession and the Islanders were hopelessly outdistanced. This was the Tigers' third win in a row and their joy was unbounded. Despite the local team's defeat, it had been a good game and the exhilaration of the crowd added to the party atmosphere that was sweeping the town.

Later, downtown at the Empress Vaudeville Theatre, The Incomparable Albini[4] dazzled the crowds with his card tricks, while comic tramps Heeley and Meeley waited in the wings. Singers Bessie Cook, Jennie Ward and William Cullen would soon follow with the ever-popular Joe Cook, blackface dancer and juggler extraordinaire. With all this frivolity fuelled by alcohol, fights were common and they always attracted a crowd, though the local constables quickly dispersed combatants and spectators alike. As the evening wore on, the merrymakers moved from one amusement to another and, as usual, some men hired a canoe and paddled up The Gorge to continue their party. Even later, there was still a place of amusement open where groups of men would be welcome, provided a certain decorum was exhibited: Stella's house.

The Saanich police at The Gorge were having trouble keeping things orderly. Over the summer there had been many incidents in the park; assaults, drunkenness, vandalism and theft had kept the force hopping and their complaints about needing more manpower went unheeded. Recently, an organized theft ring had been operating successfully in the area. It was a busy time and this weekend would prove particularly challenging: several constables who would normally have been on patrol were occupied, receiving instructions for a secret police action to take place on the stroke of midnight.

Over at Stella's place the evening was proceeding with just the right atmosphere. Attention to detail was important. She had brought in eight girls to work that night, all attractive young women wearing expensive, revealing gowns. This was her upmarket house and the prices reflected that; her Herald Street operation was more relaxed. Although she had offers, she never made herself available to the customers, as that would undermine her authority with the girls. She had enough to do, with meeting the clients, keeping the accounts and watching the help.

A local musician, Freddy Cole, played the piano, banging out the popular tunes of the day such as "By the Light of the Silvery Moon" and a selection of ragtime favourites with his usual accomplished style. Quong was in the kitchen ready to prepare any meal that was required. The liquor cellar was well stocked, with everything from beer to champagne. A knock sounded at the door and Stella swept over to the entrance to greet her guests. The baseball game was over and the Tacoma Tigers tumbled noisily in, high on their recent success and with plenty of money to spend.

"Company, ladies," Stella announced, in the time-honoured phrase that meant clients. A round of drinks was called for; introductions were made and as the evening wore on, Freddy's songs became increasingly risqué. Inevitably some wag who had just come from the vaudeville house had a couple of jokes to pass around:

In 1911 the Tacoma Tigers baseball team celebrated its triumph over the Victoria Islanders at Stella's place. Unfortunately for them, the party ended abruptly when the police raided Rockwood. [DAVE ESKENAZI COLLECTION]

(A buxom girl drops her purse, and a comic tries politely to return it.)

COMIC: I beg your pardon?

GIRL: What the hell are you begging for? You're old enough to ask for it!

(A minister walks up to a beautiful woman.)

MINISTER: Do you believe in the hereafter?

WOMAN: I certainly do!

MINISTER: (leering) Then you know what I am here after!

Not missing a beat, Freddy chimed in with an old sing-along favourite:

I went to a ball dressed as a map of France
Said a girl, show me how the French advance
When she reached the firing line I shouted in alarm
And another little drink wouldn't do us any harm.

Stella was happy with this song—it always got the drink orders moving. Her own taste ran to opera.

The unbounded merriment hid the distant shuffle of heavy footsteps on the front porch and the terse, whispered orders. There came another knock on the door—this one loud and insistent—and in walked several members of the Saanich police force supplemented by several constables on loan from Victoria.

Moments later, the girls were dressed in their day clothes while charges of being inmates of a bawdy house were read out to them. The men lined up to have their names taken and, like naughty schoolboys, were sent on their way with a warning. Freddy slipped out the back and took off in his little coupe. Quong kept silent, head down; this was all routine to him. Freddy and Quong didn't have to worry because the police knew their role in the household. The real prize was Stella, who held her ground in the confusion around her, attempting to quiet the dogs and barely managing to restrain her fury.

A few days later, as the defendant stood in the dock, she felt the years of frustration and anger wash over her. Tod Aikman, the prosecutor, walked across to Magistrate George

Jay and handed him papers detailing added charges. Jay's own frustration was clearly etched on his face.

This was the final straw. Stella was exhausted and the stump of her leg was aching from the constant rubbing of the crude wooden replacement. It wasn't long before she lost what little control she had been trying to hang on to. In a full-blown rage, exhibiting the temper she had become famous for, she banged her handbag against the rail and shouted, "Robbers, thieves, grafters!"[5] Moments later she was hustled out of the courtroom to serve a 24-hour contempt-of-court charge imposed by Magistrate Jay, who was not in the mood for any disruption.

An unidentified couple in one of the parlours at Rockwood. Leather chairs, lace and velvet drapes, silver vases with fresh flowers from the garden—Stella insisted on the very best. [PRIVATE COLLECTION]

As Jay waited for the court to settle down, he thought back to the lieutenant-governor's garden party on the weekend. He and Aikman had chatted and nibbled their way through the genteel festivities with the likes of Premier and Mrs. McBride and Chief Justice Gordon Hunter, whose wife had made quite a splash in her embroidered brown chiffon dress. The other ladies, also costumed in fine, lace-trimmed silk, satin and chiffon gowns topped with elegant picture hats, hoped for a mention in the newspapers. For the most part they were successful in attracting this attention, but what amused Jay was that another group of "smartly dressed, but heavily veiled ladies" had also made the papers.[6] Stella's girls, who had been through his courtroom that morning, were also known for their fine sense of fashion.

The Conservative Party picnic at Goldstream Park was coming up and Jay thought it would be a good idea to make an appearance. Aikman would be there and having him as an ally was essential to getting rid of this frightful woman, Stella, who was too clever for her own good. Before he retired from this bench he would see her gone from Victoria.

A few hours later, while high society gossiped about who and what had been seen at the garden party, Stella sat in jail, her thoughts racing as she massaged the stump of her leg. She would beat this as she had every other time. They don't send ladies to jail—surely it was just the usual harassment, a small setback, and she'd be back in business by the end of the week. She had to face facts, though: this time it seemed different. The sick, nervous feeling in her stomach wasn't the aftermath of too much rich food, alcohol and rage. It was what they called a "gut feeling," and hers was saying there was trouble ahead.

All too well she remembered last July and the look in Aikman's eyes as he prosecuted her for selling liquor without a licence. He stated then that this was only the first step in the campaign to rid the district of the habitués and occupants of her house. It didn't seem fair—after all, who knew more about her business operations than Tod Aikman? As her former lawyer he had got her off every time; now—the traitor—he was on the other side.

On Saturday, the Tacoma Tigers once again played the Islanders and once again they won. This game, however, was described as tame and uninteresting and it may be suspected that the teams were feeling a little the worse for wear. In contrast the Saanich police constables were still on the tear, having tracked down The Gorge theft ring: two youths, aged 17 and 14, were found with their loot in the disused schooner *Mascot*, anchored under the Point Ellice Bridge.[7] In a later court appearance, Freddy Cole managed to beat a charge of driving at excessive speed. A coupe with his number plate had been spotted in the early hours careering toward town.

The weekend was over, the town settled back into a peaceful routine, and Stella was left to reflect on where her life was going.

Two

*Foolish Misses Loose [sic] Their Kisses
in a Free and Easey [sic] Way*

O N OCTOBER 23, 1872, Uncle Billy strutted around town receiving congratulations from his neighbours. Tilly, the wife of his eldest son, Ben, had just given birth to their first child; Estella Hannah Carroll (called Stella by her mother) was Uncle Billy's first grandchild. Her second name was for Ben's mother, Uncle Billy's first wife, Hannah.

"Uncle Billy" Carroll was one of the most prominent citizens of Bourbon, Missouri. Not that this was difficult as the population rarely fluctuated above 30. He had arrived in Missouri from Tennessee when he was 16 years old and in 1842 made his way to Crawford County, took up land in and around the village of Bourbon, built a log house and married Hannah Chapman.[1] She died in 1857, leaving Uncle Billy

with two sons, Benjamin, four, and Dennis, two. The following year he married Elizabeth Burnett, with whom he raised a
family. They divorced in 1874, creating quite a scandal.
Uncle Billy was married for the third and final time to
Araminta Edington, who was his companion until his death
in 1905.

Ben and Dennis worked alongside their father but as the
land on the farm was not suitable for growing crops, most of
their effort was put toward raising stock. This was where Ben
excelled and it gave him the opportunity to move around to
other communities. Dennis was less enamoured of this work
and eventually left with his family to live in nearby St. Louis.

Ben loved to be on the move, drinking with the boys and
looking over potential livestock. He was a virile young man
with a weakness for a pretty face, particularly anyone with
small, fine features and an air of innocence. He was young
himself but he had learned the ways of the cowboys, and
many a local girl had succumbed to his flattering ways and
good looks.

On a trip to Benton, Missouri, he spotted a young woman
who seemed out of place with her fine clothes and particular
manners. Anna Mathilda "Tilly" Arms had been born in New
York. It was said she came from a well-to-do line and even was
heir to some property in New York, but her family had moved
to Benton, and she was a little put out at having to adjust to
so abrupt a change in her circumstances.

Despite her best efforts to be aloof, she was quite taken
with the handsome Ben Carroll and in November 1871 they
were married. A year later she gave birth to Stella, then Minnie

Stella's father, Benjamin Franklin Carroll, was well known for his love of pretty women and alcohol.
[PRIVATE COLLECTION]

Isabella in 1874, followed by Roy Harvey in 1878 and finally Harry Henry in 1883.[2] However, Tilly was not cut out for the hard work and difficult living conditions of the region.

There were areas of natural beauty but the land was poor. Many people were discouraged and just accepted their poverty, looking for any small pleasure they could find. Some years earlier a government agriculture report had characterized the region as inhabited by barefoot, shiftless individuals who prized their stills and "possum rifles higher than their crops." The author couldn't resist an arrogant but poetic stab at the people of the region:

Until our people [Crawford County] are educated up to the point where they can value a sheep higher than a dog, and agriculture and manufactures better than opossum and coon hunting, I suppose our crops of nutritious grains will grow to "waste their fragrance on the desert air," and our rapid streams send their babbling waters to cool the mean whiskey ... instead of making cheap clothing for our ragged people.[3]

Descriptions like this came to stereotype the inhabitants of the Ozarks, while unfairly minimizing the hardships they

Stella's mother, Tilly (Arms) Carroll, found life in the Missouri Ozarks with four children and an alcoholic husband just too much to endure.
[PRIVATE COLLECTION]

faced. The area became known for "poverty, backwardness and conservatism."[4]

By 1880 things had improved, as Bourbon was a station on the newly constructed Atlantic & Pacific Railroad and boasted a hotel, two general stores, a blacksmith and two physicians to serve the residents of the surrounding area.[5] Although the Carrolls were rather better off than many of their neighbours, the daily exposure to the struggle against poverty became their driving force to achieve a better life.

When they didn't have to do chores, Stella, Minnie and Roy enjoyed exploring the countryside. Just south of the town, in a valley bounded by steep limestone hills, was a natural spring of clear blue water, called appropriately the Blue Springs. This was the local swimming hole and with a picnic lunch, the children would be off to meet their friends, dragging little Harry with them to give their exhausted and depressed mother a break. For the truly adventurous older children there was the Meramec River with its network of caves, although dire warnings had been issued about the dangers of wandering off, never to be found again.[6] The rugged landscape gave way to meadows of wildflowers and cool glades, providing an idyllic setting for carefree childhood adventures.

This was infinitely better than being confined to their school, a two-storey, barn-like structure with the classroom on the ground floor and a meeting room above. They preferred romping around the countryside but Tilly and Uncle Billy wanted them educated. In fact, Uncle Billy had donated some of his own land and was a leader in seeing that Bourbon's first school was built, hoping that an education would

The first school in Bourbon, Missouri, which the children attended in the 1880s, was built in 1875 on land donated by Stella's grandfather. Forty pupils were taught by two teachers. It was replaced in 1895, one year after this photograph was taken. [PRIVATE COLLECTION]

give his grandchildren the means of improving their lot in life. It was the first step in opening their eyes to the wider world around them. Education was valued in the Carroll family; by the turn of the century Stella's cousin William was the county's school commissioner.[7]

For Tilly, life was not proceeding as idyllically as she had imagined when she married. Ben was a heavy drinker, away much of the time, and fragile Tilly was worn down raising four active children, supplementing the family income as a seamstress and running a household on very little money.

Her health began to suffer and she had thoughts of leaving to seek refuge with her sister, who was married to a merchant in St. Louis. Ben had other plans. With the railway going through there were reports of a land boom in southern Kansas and he was determined that a fresh start was what they needed. However, in late 1886 Tilly packed up and went to her sister's.

Not much later she was in the hospital with a respiratory ailment, possibly pneumonia. In November, a month after her 14th birthday, Stella travelled to St. Louis to visit her. As Tilly had missed Stella's birthday in October she wanted to give her eldest daughter a keepsake; she was all too aware that she would probably not be around much longer. Enlisting her sister's help, she had obtained a fine autograph book bound in deep red leather with a design of flowers and birds embossed in gold. To one side of the cover there was a small round portrait of a beautiful young girl, her golden hair curling around her shoulders and topped with a hat and turquoise ostrich feather. It was a lovely gift for her eldest daughter, a special memento. On the inside cover she wrote:

> To My Darling Stella—On your red lips, my love, lingered a smile. Though friends may flatter—Though life be gay, Do Not Forget Me When I'm Far Away. From TAC. From Mama.[8]

Stella was thrilled with the gift and could not wait to pass it around to her friends at home. She didn't fully appreciate just how significant her visit was: Tilly died in March 1887, a mere four months after this exchange. She was buried in the old cemetery in St. Louis,[9] but Stella and the rest of the family

Stella's autograph book, a gift for her 14th birthday from her mother, Tilly. It became her most prized possession, and she kept it with her all through her life. [PRIVATE COLLECTION]

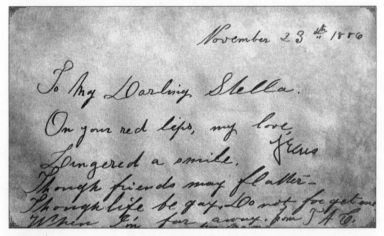

The inscription her mother wrote in her book in 1886 never failed to bring tears to Stella's eyes and put her in a reflective mood. [PRIVATE COLLECTION]

were long gone, following their erratic father who was anxious to flee painful memories.

The increasing number of people packing up and heading for Kansas was all the impetus Ben needed to gather the children and a few belongings and follow. This was a rash move on his part for a number of reasons, not the least of which was his decision to leave in the late fall. Although there was much optimism about settling in west Kansas, there were also some dire indications that life would not be easy. In January 1886, Kansas had experienced by far the worst blizzard of its recorded history and several settlers succumbed to the freezing temperatures, while their cattle froze to death in the fields. It was a terrible worry for the Carrolls to have Ben and his family leave with so little preparation, but he would not be dissuaded.

The move was chaotic and emotional for the children. They were leaving not only their dying mother, but also their grand-parents, aunts, uncles and cousins to go off to an uncertain future with an unpredictable father. The family made a concen-trated effort to keep in touch, particularly Minnie, who wrote faithfully to her cousins and returned several times to visit, but there was a pronounced strain between Uncle Billy and Ben. Some years later Ben did go back to see his father and was welcomed home. He and his brother sat on Uncle Billy's wide veranda, next to his rocking chair, and had their picture taken; Dennis, who had chosen to stay close to home, looking cool and relaxed, Ben, who hadn't, looking awkward and uncomfortable.

Fear of the unknown aside, the move west was an exciting and even thrilling experience for adventurous children like the Carrolls. It was a lively time in Kansas. The sparsely settled southwest region was experiencing growth and development totally foreign to that point. In 1886 the aptly named weekly newspaper the *Garden City Irrigator* quoted a 55-year-old man by the name of Worrell on his establishment of a successful cattle operation. According to Worrell he had travelled the whole western half of the continent but found "no place where a poor man can settle down and get rich on as little capital as right here in Western Kansas."[10]

Stories and testimonials from individuals like Worrell were everywhere and hopeful land seekers poured into the territory by train, wagon, buggy, horseback and foot. Some were young people, looking for a place to start; some were

Stella's grandfather, known as Uncle Billy, her father, Ben, and Ben's brother, Dennis, on the porch in Bourbon, Missouri. Uncle Billy was considered one of Bourbon's finest citizens. [PRIVATE COLLECTION]

older, looking for a change. And moving along with this tide of humanity came Ben Carroll with his four children. Stella, when not otherwise occupied, kept an eye on Minnie, 10, Roy, 8, and 3-year-old Harry.

Stella at 14 was adjusting to the fact that she was now the senior female in the family. Due to their father's restless behaviour, she took on the role of her siblings' protector, and Minnie, ever a nurturing soul, became the mother; they followed these roles in varying degrees for the rest of their lives. Their shared hardship and experience bonded the four children in a profound way. Although they eventually moved on to follow their own paths, they never lost touch and would drop everything in a second if one of them needed help. For now, however, this kind of responsibility was a heavy burden, and like teenaged girls through the ages, Stella was occupied with romantic dreams. She was already sneaking out to meet boys when the opportunity presented itself.

Though she felt deeply the loss of her mother, for Stella the move to Kansas was exhilarating and full of adventure. It was her first experience in a new environment, and there were lots of people to meet, especially and most importantly boys. Stella had already acquired a strong, shapely body, wavy hair and well-balanced features much like her mother's. She was not as pretty as Minnie, who was developing womanly curves of her own, a fact which kept a sisterly jealousy simmering under the surface. What Stella did have was another quality that came from her mother, an air of refinement. Combined with her mischievous, bawdy sense of humour, it produced a strong sexual appeal.

Children raised on farms knew first-hand all about sex, just from witnessing animal life and livestock breeding. Pretty young girls soon learned to stay away from cowboys who were quick to tease and fondle, unless of course the interest was mutual. Sex and alcohol were the most important and sought-after pleasures for a large part of the population, and young women who chose to ignore high moral principles were free to indulge their pleasure-seeking as well.

Part child and part woman, Stella charmed many and passed her precious little autograph book around to friends, both male and female, who responded by writing the usual funny, poetic and trite comments that have been popular through the ages. One young man by the name of Powells, who came completely under her spell, wrote of the devotion and turmoil of young love:

> *Jan. 9th, 1887*
> *Dear Estella*
> *I'll prove as constant as a dove*
> *If you will prove the same my love*
> *What the duce can be the matter*
> *For in my heart there's such a clatter*
> *Yours with kindest regards,*
> *P. M. Powells* [11]

Stella later claimed P. M. Powells was her first sweetheart, but he was only a storekeeper and she had greater ambitions. Another admirer was a man named Kirsey, who lived in Garden City, Kansas. Stella counted him as one of her beaux and said he was "sweet" to her, but he too was left by the wayside.

It was an early lesson in how valuable her attractiveness could be, particularly when men far outnumbered young women.

Garden City was a centre of activity. It had a U.S. Land Office and nowhere was optimism about growth and prosperity more evident. The Atchison, Topeka & Santa Fe rail line came right into town where, it was said, nearly everybody disembarked. The town grew so rapidly that the adjacent prairie was a sea of tents and covered wagons as men made their way daily to the Land Office to file claims. The town boomed. A streetcar ran right down the main street—five cents a ride. When a faucet was turned on, water came out. When the sun went down, streetlights came on. Seemingly overnight, hotels went up and businesses opened. Lumberyards, stores, public buildings and even an opera house appeared in short order. The streets were crowded with every mode of transportation from teams of oxen to horse and buggy. There was no comparison to Bourbon; this was how life should be.

The Carrolls were not in a position to move into town yet, and their most immediate concern was to have a roof over their heads while they surveyed the possibilities for settlement. Like many of their transient neighbours, they built a sod house. Everyone had to pitch in; sod strips were cut from the prairie soil and grass and, with help from other newcomers, they soon had shelter. Stella found that it was insulated and fireproof but aside from that it was miserable. And it leaked.

One particular rainy night Minnie awoke to find streams of mud seeping down the walls and along the floor. Knowing from experience what this could lead to, she woke the other children and together they did their best to keep the walls patched. Non-stop heavy rain meant the house could collapse, burying them underneath, and they had to stay awake and alert to this possible disaster. It had happened to other settlers and lives were lost.

Finally the rain let up. Though the sun appeared, the roof dripped for days and the children were left frantically pushing their beds around the small room to keep dry, and placing every pan they had to catch the drips. It became a hilarious game for Roy and little Harry but for the girls, who were going to have to wash everything anyway, it was infuriating. They had their mother's genteel nature and had tried to make the damp, dark and depressing place into a home. This experience had a lasting effect: Stella was determined that from then on, she would live in decent, even luxurious, houses.

Stella charmed as much material as she could from Powells at the store. They hung sacking on pegs to conceal the rough walls and ceiling and to keep out drafts. They covered the cold dirt floor with bits of carpeting and made pillows from dishcloths to soften the hard, home-built furniture. They set up their most precious possession—their mirror— and artfully draped a scarf across it. What heat they had came from a stove fuelled with dried buffalo or cow manure, and the light was produced by coal-oil lamps. Needless to say, the smell was overwhelming. The boys were enlisted to collect prairie flowers to put in a jar for a bright note in the dreary, dim light. The house was tolerable but never comfortable, and hardships like these only steeled Stella's and Minnie's resolve to possess the finer things in life, things that the wealthy landowning people had.

As if this wasn't bad enough, Kansas had more than its share of creeping and crawling creatures to plague the settlers. While Stella was off using her feminine wiles to charm the local lads, Minnie kept her brothers amused with the rhymes of a local poet, Frank Baker:

> *How happy I feel when I crawl into bed,*
> *And a rattlesnake rattles a tune at my head,*
> *And the gay little centipede void of all fear,*
> *Crawls over my neck and down into my ear,*
> *And the gay little bedbugs, so cheerful and bright,*
> *They keep me a-laughing two-thirds of the night,*
> *And the gay little flea with sharp tacks on his toes,*
> *Plays "Why don't you catch me" all over my nose.*[12]

Rattlesnakes were plentiful and known to drop through the roof without much notice. Everyone checked their boots closely before pulling them on in case one had chosen to nest in a warm place, and snakebite remedies were always kept close at hand.

It was a dangerous existence, with newcomers and itinerant wanderers passing through on a daily basis. Any female alone was at risk of molestation and rape. Warm-hearted, friendly Minnie was particularly vulnerable when the rest of the family had gone into the town. On one occasion a drunken stranger deduced that the 11-year-old girl was on her own and attempted to force himself on her. It was a difficult situation, but the familiar Carroll temperament took hold and he was quickly rousted with a cast-iron frying pan aimed strategically at his head.[13]

Work for Ben was plentiful, with both irrigation schemes

and railroad building reaching a peak of activity. By 1888 the total rail mileage was 8,779, the majority constructed in the previous three years.[14] What had once been a region of cow towns was rapidly being transformed by settlement.

It was just a few years earlier that Dodge City had been infamous for its rough population, where the soon-to-be legends of the Old West, Wyatt Earp and Bat Masterson, had dispensed frontier justice. For eight-year-old Roy, it was the Wild West and, caught up in the excitement, he wrote in his sister's autograph book, "Stella the first I ever wrote was Bad Boy I think the last will be Cow Boy."[15] In the 1880s, "cow boy," always written as two words, was synonymous with criminal and villain. A cow boy was a tough, uneducated and uncultured individual given to carousing, heavy drinking and violence. Within 10 years this had changed into one word, "cowboy," and denoted a "romantic title for so-called knights on horseback, with not the slightest taint of the pejorative," an image that continues today.[16] For Roy, the term had already begun to take on this exciting aspect and it was something he wanted to be a part of. He soon learned that following the rules was not the way things were done in the Wild West.

By 1889 the initial boom in Kansas was over, and as fast as they came the settlers packed up and left. There was a new opportunity on the horizon: free land up for grabs in the Oklahoma Territory. Not surprisingly, this free land came at a cost to others. Originally it had been negotiated away from the Creek and Seminole tribes for other displaced peoples, such as the Cherokee, who had been pushed off their own traditional lands. The pro-settlement people or "boomers" argued that the land had really not been used by the tribes and that it should now be opened to land seekers. A quick monetary agreement was reached, a government bill amended and the "unassigned lands" were available for the taking. As there were many more potential pioneers than claims a competition was organized.

April 22, 1889, was a clear, bright spring day heralding a new beginning. The would-be settlers, men, women and children, literally lined up along the borders of the unassigned lands in order to rush in, stakes in hand, to claim the best piece they could. Those seeking land farther in sat on their wagons, buggies and horses waiting for the signal for the mad dash. Among those on horses were Ben and Roy. Not far behind were Stella and Minnie with little Harry wedged between them in their wagon. The cavalry guns and cannons went off and the race was on.

Ben and Roy rushed in with everyone else and it wasn't long before they spied land that seemed right for them. They grabbed their stakes, measured out a quarter section and were about to proceed with the physical staking of their property when a couple of strangers rode up to inform them that they had already claimed it. These men had skirted the cavalry guards and "jumped the gun." With his young son at his side, Ben began to argue the unfairness of breaking the rules, but when the men pulled out their guns he had to leave and find another place to stake.[17] It was a dramatic event in the life of young Roy and one he would never forget. Sadly, it was an incident that was repeated many times throughout the area. The cheaters became known as "sooners" and their actions, coupled with the almost impossible task of sorting out who got where first, tied up the courts with land-claim disputes for years.

Stella and Minnie fared better. They chose a quarter section, hammered in their stakes and then spread their wagon sheet on the ground and sat down. No man dared to challenge the two feisty young girls, something Ben had counted on.

Ben's claim, the second one he and Roy found, was in a town that was developing along the rail line. It was known originally as Santa Fe but later renamed Newkirk. Stella had taken out a claim out there too and enlisted her father's hired hands to build a proper house for her and the other children. Finally, they could escape from the sod house. As Ben's

Ben Carroll and his partner, Paris, established a livery stable in Newkirk, Oklahoma, shortly after participating in the Oklahoma Land Rush. In this photo, Ben is standing in the doorway on the left, facing sideways. [PRIVATE COLLECTION]

expertise and interest was in livestock, he set up a livery stable with a partner named Paris.

This business kept him away from Newkirk for days and even weeks at a time. Sometimes the children travelled with him to New Mexico, Arizona and California, where they learned about the new frontier. They were to see that above all, entrepreneurship was the most valued trait and high-profit businesses the most desirable investment. As there were more cowboys than families in these towns, the businesses that developed first were those that met their needs. Hotels, restaurants, saloons, gambling houses and brothels were in demand and that was where money was to be made. The owners of these enterprises became the local elite, and despite their sometimes dubious activities they gained a sort of romantic respectability. Stella, observant and bright, saw such people as models, guides to the way out of mortifying poverty.

Now a daring and flirtatious young woman of 16, Stella would openly meet a man's admiring glance and return it with a wink. She was confident in her feminine power and not hesitant to use it. Smart, strong and attractive, she knew exactly what she wanted and how to get it. She liked to listen in on the men's conversations and was as determined to make her way in the world as they were. She was already used to handling her father's business affairs; he knew livestock but because of his drinking habit, he was not capable of dealing with the finances. She was clever enough to see that there were boundless opportunities in these railway towns and that acquiring and developing land produced profits. Some of her better-placed male friends were quite taken with her spirited

Stella (right)
with sister
Minnie and
brother Roy.
[PRIVATE
COLLECTION]

ways and it amused them to educate her in business in exchange for her girlish attention. While she could play the fragile teenager, she was brimming with the confidence of youth. She felt that she was in control and it was a feeling she would not, and indeed could not, ever surrender.

Stella became a busy young woman, extracting favours from the men she came across and getting caught up in the land development that was spawned by the railroad. The excitement of actually owning her own property encouraged her to want more. She was resolved to see her sister and brothers educated and even little Harry had to show his writing skill in Stella's now slightly worn but still precious autograph book:

> *To Stella*
> *When if ever a man I'll be and this I see & say why sister whose writing is this. Harry Carl [sic] I am on the bed writering [sic].*[18]

Stella was not at home much anymore; she preferred to be out and around the town, flirting with bankers, shopkeepers and railway officials while artfully ignoring the admiring glances of the cowboys who frequented her father's livery stable. Minnie was frustrated at being left at home to care for the boys and cook for their father, though her sister was undeniably good at bringing home little gifts she had beguiled out of hopeful men. She knew Stella was a little too bold, but with their mother gone and their father occupied elsewhere, no one particularly cared, and Minnie could see that Stella was having fun. Childhood innocence had become the latest luxury they could not afford.

Stella's youngest brother, Harry Henry Carroll, at about age nine. The mischievous one in the family, he was quite dapper in later life. The suit he is wearing in this photograph was undoubtedly Stella's idea. [PRIVATE COLLECTION]

Three

Live For Those That Love You,
   For Those Whose Hearts Are True

ETWEEN CAREFUL PROPERTY development and an even more careful selection of boyfriends, Stella was beginning to prosper. By 1894 she had moved to Gallup, New Mexico, with Minnie and her brothers, and purchased a house for them to live in. Admiring men quickly surrounded her and on November 19 she married Dudley Walter Curtis, 26, a general contractor who was living in Winslow, Arizona.[1] She rented her Gallup house and moved the family to Arizona. Both Gallup and Winslow were on the Atlantic & Pacific Railroad and this naturally brought growth to the towns. Stella's entrepreneurial spirit was in high gear and she continued to speculate in real estate and property development. By the time she was 25 she owned the lots and houses in Newkirk and Gallup, and six lots in Winslow that she planned to develop.

Mrs. D. W. Curtis has purchased four lots in the northeastern portion of the city, and intends building neat brick cottages on them for renting purposes. Mrs. Curtis is one of Winslow [*sic*] most enterprising citizens and it is a pity we have not more like her.[2]

It filled Stella with pride to see herself described as an enterprising citizen. It would probably put Dudley in one of his sulking moods, but she was secretly pleased to be noticed in this way. She knew her own worth and was not about to hide behind any man while he took credit for her accomplishments.

In fact, she had managed to turn what two weeks ago had appeared to be a disaster into an advantage. On June 6, she received word that a fire had swept through part of Gallup and

Residence Street, Winslow, Ariz.

A street in Winslow, Arizona, in 1918. During the 1890s, Stella was a major developer of residential property here. [PRIVATE COLLECTION]

among the losses were her house and all its furniture. She privately congratulated herself on her foresight in heavily insuring that property; the settlement in turn gave her the capital to buy the lots in Winslow. She then sold the lot in Gallup and consolidated her property investments in Winslow.

With her eye for property and Dudley's work as a contractor they seemed a good match, but the reality behind closed doors was quite different. Shortly after they married Stella discovered that Dudley was horribly jealous of any attention she gave or received. She was amassing a considerable amount of money now and decided it would be best if she sent 18-year-old Minnie to a convent school in Santa Clara, California, to earn a teaching certificate and put the boys, now aged 15 and 11, into a private boarding school in San Jose run by a strict but rather emotional woman with the aristocratic name of Mrs. Von Bendeleben. She wanted to see them educated but was worried about Dudley's outbursts and the fact that the children always rushed to her aid. He would be easier to handle without them around and it would be good for them to start preparing for a future independent of her.

<hr />

In San Jose, on a typical Sunday morning, Mrs. Von Bendeleben was bustling around, fussing over "her boys" in their haphazard efforts to get ready for Sunday School. Roy, the eldest, looked on wearily, also anxious to get the boys moving but for quite a different reason. Harry was larking about as usual, making everyone laugh and severely disrupting

Minnie and Stella. Minnie was sent to a convent school to earn a teaching certificate, but she had other career ideas. [PRIVATE COLLECTION]

the efforts of the proper school mistress, who dispensed the collection money in a final attempt to get the pups out the door. Roy, in his quiet manner, took charge and off they set. Once out of sight of the house he pulled them to one side of the walk and put out his hand; the boys dutifully deposited in it their share of the coins for the collection plate. It was their weekly ritual. Roy loped into the store for his Bull Durham tobacco and rolling papers, and penny candy to keep his charges quiet. He had learned to roll his own cigarettes from watching the cowboys at his father's livery stable and continued to do so for the rest of his life. Mrs. Von Bendeleben was never the wiser.

Roy and Harry were both good-looking and well liked, Roy as quiet and taciturn in nature as Harry was playful and talkative. Stella made sure they were well dressed and intended to give them a good start in life. They did not stay long with Mrs. V., much to her disappointment, as her fondness for Harry in particular was evident. Shortly before Christmas in 1894 the boys returned to Stella's house in Winslow. On December 19, Mrs. Von Bendeleben, dabbing at her eyes with her fine linen handkerchief, wrote in Harry's autograph book:

> *Dear Harry*
> *God Bless you, dear boy, through all your journey's [sic] of life!*
> *And may you become a blessing and comfort to your loving sister,*
> *Stella; and sometimes think of your many friends in California.*
> *Ever, Your true friend & teacher*
> *Mrs. H. Von Bendeleben*[3]

Roy eventually returned to work for his father, while Harry was enrolled for a time at St. John's Lutheran College in Winfield, Kansas. He studied Latin, tried pre-med courses and even started in law. But nothing seemed to stick and he was just another young man who appeared to have means and liked a good time. An attractive young woman, egged on by her avaricious family, inveigled Harry into a hastily arranged marriage. Either they were unaware of, or were underestimating, Harry's oldest sister. As soon as Stella got wind of this she stormed back to Kansas, had the marriage annulled and whisked Harry off to Europe.

Minnie's fortunes were about to turn at this time too. She had stayed at the convent in Santa Clara and obtained a teaching

Stella's brothers, Roy and Harry, grew up to be handsome and personable young men. [PRIVATE COLLECTION]

certificate. A portrait taken at this time shows a pretty young woman with large brown eyes, fair skin and thick, wavy hair. She was small in stature, only five foot two, but possessed an hourglass figure, a very sought-after silhouette for a young woman. She is wearing a ruffled, elaborately trimmed dress and holding a fan. This is in contrast to Stella's portrait, taken the same year, in which she is dressed in a tailored and fitted suit, a tastefully trimmed hat and leather gloves and is clutching, most appropriately, what appears to be a small leather wallet. Minnie was always the soft, pretty sister; Stella the handsome, self-confident one.

Minnie might have led a different life had she become a teacher but she fell in love with an older man who persuaded

Stella loved the idea of being a businesswoman and dressed the part when she visited San Francisco in 1894.
[PRIVATE COLLECTION]

Minnie in 1894.
She had a
girlish air of
innocence and
beauty that
captivated
many men—
including
married ones.
[PRIVATE
COLLECTION]

her, with promises of marriage, to run away to San Francisco with him. The marriage never took place—he may have been married already—and Minnie was now a "fallen woman."[4] She decided to explore the highly lucrative business of prostitution. By 1898 she had moved to Albuquerque, New Mexico, where, lacking Stella's grand ambition and ready capital, she worked as a prostitute for Lizzie McGrath and operated various brothel and "wine rooms" of her own over the next few years. Much later, when old-timers reminisced about Albuquerque's red-light district, known as "hell's half acre," they remembered Lizzie as the most successful madam and Minnie as the most beautiful.

Minnie had a brothel of her own in Albuquerque, New Mexico, where she worked with another successful madam, Lizzie McGrath, who is seen here climbing a fence in front of her place, accompanied by her "sister." [PRIVATE COLLECTION]

In the meantime Stella's problems with Dudley had worsened. The couple often attended dances where Dudley felt Stella was far too familiar with other men, not appreciating that it had been the key to her success all along.

On one occasion he pulled her off the dance floor, insisting that they leave. At home in bed, Stella, thinking Dudley was finally calm, asked him why he was so jealous. He rose up in bed, ranting and calling her "vile" names and began choking her. Hearing her screams, a neighbour, Mrs. Giles, and a passerby, Charley Hawkins, broke into the room in time to witness Dudley yelling, "If I had a gun I would kill you." Charley Hawkins described the scene:

> When I was going home from the ball being held at the Machine Shops in Winslow, Arizona, at between two and three o'clock in the morning I was going by Curtis's house [and] heard someone hallow [sic] "this man is killing me ... " I ... opened the door and went in lit a match and recognized Mr. & Mrs. Curtis. Mrs. Curtis sitting on the edge of the bed he Mr. Curtis was standing by her side with one hand on her throat ... he told me to get out of his house. I walked to the door turned around and Mrs. Curtis [ran] towards me. Mr. Curtis followed her caught her by the hair of her head and slammed the door shut and then I went home.[5]

Stella had to conceal the black-and-blue finger marks on her neck for some time.

Dudley's evil temper wasn't confined to Stella. He was arrested and charged on December 28 with felonious assault and attempted murder on the person of John Denair, who worked for the railroad. Curtis had fired his pistol, wounding Denair. He was released two days later on $1,000 bail.[6]

In May 1896, Dudley and Stella travelled to Oklahoma to attend the marriage of her father, Ben, aged 41, to a Cherokee woman named Mattie Martin, 20 years younger.[7] On the way back they stopped in Gallup and another violent incident ensued when Dudley verbally attacked Stella in the street, threatening her life, and throwing her down to kick her.

Back in Winslow the following month, attendance at another community dance occasioned the last and worst of these attacks. It started benignly enough; Dudley crossed the floor and formally asked Stella to dance. They joined a set of other dancers but before long, he began to rant about Stella's flirting with another man. He pulled out his pocketknife and said, "If you smile or wink at him again I will cut your throat." He then ordered her to get her things and come home with him. They were just out of the hall when he began raving again and struck her in the face with his fist. She managed to break free, run back and get Charley Hawkins to summon the constable, who took Dudley into custody for the night.

He was released in the morning long enough to return to the house and threaten Stella again, but was finally arrested by the sheriff for breaking his bond on his criminal charges. He was placed in the jail in the nearby town of Holbrook but eluded his jailer after they had been out for dinner. He apparently fled the territory and was not seen again.[8]

Stella at the
time of her
marriage to
Dudley Curtis
in 1894.
[PRIVATE
COLLECTION]

In July Stella filed for divorce based on Dudley's mistreatment of her and the fact she had been supporting him, to the point of even paying his lodge dues. She claimed all the personal property and household furniture, and all the real estate holdings, which were in her name anyway. She put her newly furnished, eight-room boarding house up for sale, but once again she was the victim of a fire when it nearly burned down just a few days later. The newspapers reported the origin of the fire as a "mystery," as the room where it started was unoccupied at the time. When the door was broken open the bed and carpet were on fire; had the blaze got out of control the entire business section of Winslow could have been lost.

Four days after Stella's divorce hearing, she left for California.

Mrs. W.D. [sic] Curtis left on No.1 last Wednesday afternoon for Southern California, to be gone about six weeks or two months. Her health has run down considerable, and she proposes to take a needed rest to try and recuperate.[9]

Not long after her return she put her own home up for sale. The ad described it as one of the finest residences in Winslow, complete with the best and most modern furniture. She then purchased another place, as she wasn't quite ready to leave Winslow yet. Another man had caught her eye.

On July 3, 1897, the *Winslow Mail* reported the marriage of Mrs. Estella H. Curtis to Jackson F. Durlin at the bride's residence. Stella was 25; Jackson was 34. It was a quiet wedding with a just a few friends, including the local district commissioner, W. A. Parr, who had presided over her divorce. The *Mail*, in extending its heartiest congratulations to the couple, mentioned the "bounteous luncheon and a liberal quantity of wines and liquors, which were freely partaken and thoroughly enjoyed by those present."[10] Stella looked stunning in a dark velvet gown trimmed in lace and fur with a diamond starburst pin, a gift from Jackson, placed artfully in her thick, beautiful hair. It was a short-lived marriage, however, and in less than a year Stella was on the move again.

Her trip to the west coast in 1896 had not been only for recuperative purposes. She wanted to investigate another business and she had made all the right contacts. She had been sidetracked by her marriage to Durlin, but that had quickly gone sour and she was ready for a change.

It was early 1898 before Stella was able to test her business prowess. She had finished with Durlin and it was time to prove her talents in a more sophisticated venue than the small towns she was accustomed to. Things were slowing down in Arizona; the railroad was well established, as were the towns along the way, so Stella looked to the great city of San Francisco. Timing was important, and it was booming.

San Francisco in the 1890s was noteworthy for many things, not the least of which was its dubious distinction as the vice capital of the coast, a reputation it had enjoyed for several decades. Particular neighbourhoods, such as the Barbary Coast and the Tenderloin, and the cosmopolitan air that pervaded the entire city drew many people seeking bright lights, good times and adventures. It was ruled by powerful political bosses and for an enterprising man or woman willing to play the game, there was money to be made.

After divorcing Curtis, Stella married Jackson Durlin in 1897; this is her wedding portrait. Note the diamond pin set in her hair. [PRIVATE COLLECTION]

A person had to have capital to get started, but Stella had money from her property-development schemes and the future looked bright. The city was like no place she had ever been. As she made her way along the foggy streets, trying to spot the house numbers, she consulted the paper in her hand. The scale of the buildings, the rapid movements of horses and carriages, and the crowded streets caused her to quicken her own steps. The wet cobblestones were slippery but she managed to keep her footing. Though she was chilled to the bone, the cold air brought with it a sense of excitement. This was a new beginning and a new challenge, something that never failed to make her heart beat a little faster.

As an intelligent child on the frontier, Stella had realized that there was always a need for "the oldest profession," and though she was not inclined to work as a prostitute herself, the business aspect appealed to her. Brothels, high class or low, were usually run by women, at a time when there were few women in business for themselves, and the position of such madams had piqued Stella's interest. She was firm in her desire to be independent and she knew she could be successful in this field: she had a good head for financial affairs and she was accustomed to shepherding her siblings. This protectiveness could be applied to her "girls." Perhaps the strongest attraction of being an upscale madam was that a well-run house, catering to wealthy, powerful men, would have to be clean, elegant and beautifully furnished—the polar opposite of the desperately dirty and uncomfortable sod house in which her family had had to live.

Stella had heard a lot about Tessie Wall, the top madam in San Francisco, and felt they were bound to be good friends. They had both known hard times but had come through them with determination and humour. Tessie had proven her abilities by rising to the peak of her profession and operating more than one establishment catering to a genteel level of clientele. Stella could learn the important points of managing a successful house and invest in a profitable business. The type of operation she was interested in was a parlour house—a high-class house of prostitution.

If Stella was going to learn a profession from someone it might as well be the best and Tessie Wall certainly was that. Born in 1869 in the Irish working-class Mission district of San Francisco, pretty, blond Teresa Susan Donahue was one of 10 children. Through necessity she began working at menial jobs and at the age of 15 she married a local fireman, Edward Wall. The marriage was short-lived and Tessie then entered the rarefied world of the city's elite by becoming a domestic servant for a well-to-do family. It was here that she learned first-hand what a truly comfortable lifestyle could be for those with the means to attain it.

In time, Tessie grew bored with her tedious tasks and began to frequent some of the local Barbary Coast dance halls and drinking establishments. She became renowned for her capacity to consume large quantities of liquor and one memorable night, she reportedly out-drank the legendary boxer John L. Sullivan.[11] Whether that story was true or not, she was a captivating woman in both personality and looks, and she knew she had the key to improving her lot in life. The temptation to cash in on her assets for a quick return was too much to resist and within a very few years, Tessie had become the pre-eminent hostess of the city. By the late 1890s she and Stella had linked up, and Tessie became a mentor to her friend.

Prostitution was so accepted that no semblance of discretion was needed. Madam Lucy, who operated an establishment on Sacramento Street, was particularly easy to find: she had an engraved copper plate nailed to her door saying "Ye Olde Whore Shoppe." It accomplished the desired effect of attracting attention, but eventually was removed at the request of the police.[12] The women, or more commonly "girls," however old they were, were known by many terms, "daughters of joy" and "ladies of the night" being two of the more charming.

Stella was getting quite an education, not only in the fine points of madamship but also in life in all its forms in a big city. Prostitution at this time existed on many levels. The "cribs," which numbered in the hundreds, were large buildings, some specially built, with tiny cubicles containing a bed, chair and washbasin. In these cubicles women sold their bodies for from 25 cents to four dollars. The prostitute rented the cubicle and any revenue exceeding the rent was her income. The cribs were dirty, depressing and degrading, and a woman reduced to this was not likely to have a long life. It came to light many years later that the cribs provided a generous income for some corrupt politicians.

At the other end of the social scale of the demimonde was the parlour house. Life in these institutions in the 1890s was very organized, although the financial structure could vary widely. Sometimes business people capitalized them; sometimes they were partnerships or a family business. Whatever the case, the owner provided a well-situated building, tastefully decorated, with a staff on hand that could include a house-keeper, cook, maids and a doorman-cum-bouncer. The manager who oversaw the house was the madam, more often than not also the owner. Many madams started out with financial backers but because the profits could be so substantial they were soon able to operate independently.

The women of the house were employed under one of two systems: in the boarding-house arrangement, a woman would pay a certain amount for room, board and expenses and then keep her own earnings; in a percentage house the madam supplied the amenities and took anywhere from 25 to 50 percent of the earnings. The madams also made a considerable amount of money from food and liquor sales, as well as kickbacks from the local merchants in whose shops the girls were required to purchase what they needed.

The women had to maintain a certain appearance and that required a considerable outlay for the right wardrobe. Beverly Davis worked in the house of Jessie Hayman, Tessie's chief rival in San Francisco, and in her memoirs gives a complete list of what was required and the approximate costs:

1 fox fur for suit	$300.00
4 tailored suits	$100.00 each
4 street dresses	$75.00 each
8 hats for street	$15.00 each
2 coats (1 plain, 1 fur-trimmed)	$250.00 each
12 pairs street shoes	$18.00 each

4½ doz. hose	$5.00 pr
6 pocketbooks	$10.00 each
2 evening bags	$10.00 each
½ doz. gloves, street	$8.00 pr
½ doz. evening gloves	$12.50 pr
7 evening gowns	$100.00 each
7 negligees	$75.00 each
12 teddy slips	$18.00 each
24 nightgowns	$20.00 each
6 pairs mules	$15.00 each
2 evening wraps, fur trimmed	$750.00 each
7 pairs evening shoes	$15.00 each
9 doz. handkerchiefs	$11.50 doz.
6 blouses	$10.00 each
TOTAL	**$6,088.50**

The prices above are anywhere from double to as much as 10 times the amount an item would cost if bought from a catalogue or another store. Though a lot of money was made by these women, in the words of Davis, "sporting girls always pay."[13]

That was the beginning of my slant on clothes and the bank-roll needed to keep up the dizzy pace. Ratty looking women get no play from men. It's the wardrobe that lands the business. Good girls in high-priced parlour houses—and by good I mean they can keep their clients coming regularly and asking for them—have to have expensive layouts. The madams lay down the law. No outfit no work. Sherman [Hayman] went with us and did the shopping. She got the rakeoffs. We patronized certain stores that kick-backed to her house. If a girl looked like a good bet when a procurer brought her in and she didn't have the b.r [bank-roll], Sherman advanced the money for her wardrobe. Took it out of her earnings.[14]

These top-class parlour houses were where the big money was made, but for many women contemplating establishing their own operation, the competition and financial outlay was a little too rich. Most of the girls had a transitory life because police magistrates routinely imposed the restriction that they must move on. An unofficial circuit included San Francisco, Vancouver, Victoria, Seattle, Tacoma and Portland, and it was not uncommon to find prostitutes who had started in the business in the flashy Tenderloin establishments of San Francisco arrested in the other cities.[15] Women who possessed the right personality traits and business acumen, and perhaps a patron willing to bankroll them, could establish elsewhere the kind of house they had worked for in San Francisco.

Stella's investments in San Francisco worked out advanta-geously and she decided she was ready to start her own oper-ation. First, however, she would fulfill a long-held dream. Stella, Minnie and 17-year-old recently annulled Harry set off for a grand tour of Europe. They visited England, Germany, France and Ireland, where Harry lay on the parapet dangling back to kiss the Blarney Stone and lost all his loose change in the process. He hardly needed to perform this ritual to acquire eloquence. In London, they toured Westminster

Abbey and once again mischievous Harry caused a sensation when he slipped under the velvet ropes and sat upon the English throne. A roar soon erupted from an extremely upset guard who chastised him roundly with dire warnings that such a breach was punishable by death.[16]

When they weren't trying to keep irrepressible Harry in line, Stella and Minnie indulged their love of shopping, purchasing wonderful gowns, antiques, leather-bound books and even one statue of a classical nude—essential to an upscale parlour house. All these experiences increased the bond between the siblings and their attachment to each other was strengthened. Roy missed the trip, but he had big plans.

After spending some time in Oklahoma helping their father in the livery business, he couldn't wait to tell Stella of a colossal opportunity that could bring wealth to them all. Roy had "gold fever" and decided to join the throngs of men moving north for the Yukon and later Alaska gold rushes. There was an obvious opportunity for Stella here too.

When Stella returned from Europe she immediately set about searching for the perfect place to relocate and to take advantage of the quest for gold. There were several cities to choose from. San Francisco was a major outfitter for the gold seekers, but Portland, Tacoma, Seattle, Victoria and Vancouver were also doing well. They were all possible but Victoria and Vancouver were farther away and, of course, in another country. Seattle and Victoria had all the attributes of San Francisco: they were well connected to the regular transportation systems along the coast; they were near large military installations; and they were centres for shipping, sealing and whaling. Both had also gained importance as supply depots and embarkation points for the gold rushes in the north. Both were booming and Stella knew, from her experiences in Arizona, the importance of cashing in on boom towns.

San Francisco was already well served by the type of high-class establishment she envisioned, and although she visited both Portland and Tacoma, by October 1899 she was settled in Seattle, and hoping she had chosen wisely.[17] She transferred her remaining Winslow properties to her sister, who had returned to run a modest brothel in Albuquerque, New Mexico. It was conveniently on the direct rail line to Winslow, so Minnie could easily handle the rentals there.

There were plenty of miners in Seattle; it was the hub for those leaving for the Klondike as well as those who had struck it rich and were returning. Seattle also had a number of prominent madams already operating upscale places. Foremost among them was Lou Graham, a German immigrant, who had learned the business in San Francisco and, in a visionary move, had taken a chance on Seattle in its formative years. When Seattle was small, her operation was basic. As the town grew into a city and matured, her business broadened and became more sophisticated. She put in the time, cultivated community leaders and politicians and established herself as a backroom power broker.[18] Others had followed her lead with some success, but Lou was number one and Stella was not going to settle for anything less. She would have to proceed cautiously if she wished to take this position from Lou.

Roy, in the meantime, was not faring well in his quest for riches in Alaska. He did hit a small pocket of gold but it quickly petered out. He was disappointed, but only slightly; after all, the real riches lay in the adventure, the quest. But practicalities must be attended to, so he set himself up as a barber in a little tent camp near Juneau. He made more money cutting hair, giving shaves and trimming beards than he ever did prospecting, but he soon rejoined Stella in Seattle.

Stella, restless with having a status inferior to Lou Graham's, decided to go to Victoria and spend Christmas with some of her colleagues from San Francisco who were operating a successful brothel there. She may have planned this as a brief holiday but it was to have a happy, unexpected and lasting effect.

four

As We Journey Through Life—
Let Us Play By The Way

STELLA HAD A ROUGH AND chilly trip on the S.S. *Garland* across the Strait of Juan de Fuca in December 1899. At this time of year there was often fog to slow down the run, and it was just her luck that the two luxury steamers normally on this route were gone: one had been sold and the other had sunk following a collision with another ship in Tacoma Harbour.[1]

A few hours later she was restoring warmth to her body with a good shot of whisky provided by her friend Vera Ashton at her brothel in Victoria. As Stella settled in for the Christmas festivities she had no idea that this trip would change the course of her life. She was open to new opportunities and a tragedy was about to drop one into her lap.

Christmas Day at this upscale brothel, located on the suitably named Broad Street, was a pleasant and well-attended event. Two Chinese cooks prepared a sumptuous dinner with a wide selection of meats, game and poultry, vegetables, fruits and sweets, washed down with liberal amounts of spirits, wine and champagne and the merrymaking went on well into the early hours of the morning. In part the celebration was about the transfer of the brothel business from Vera to a woman known as Marval Conn.

Finally, when everyone had gone to bed, with or without a partner, Marval decided on one last drink. She was starting to feel hungry and was too keyed up to sleep. About 4:00 AM she knocked at the door of the room occupied by another visitor,

Broad Street in Victoria, B.C. Once a street of brothels and saloons, it was eventually "cleaned up" and became an area of respectable businesses and shops. [PRIVATE COLLECTION]

Dorothy Carol, and asked her if she would like to partake of a light lunch in the drawing room. Odd though it may seem, the early-morning hours were quite a normal time for the ladies of the demimonde to have lunch. Daytime was for sleeping.

Dorothy agreed and the two women parted, Dorothy going to the parlour and Marval, carrying a lamp, searching for one of her favourite treats, leftover turkey. She returned a short time later "much put out" at not finding any, so Dorothy returned to her room, leaving Marval alone in the drawing room. Later, Dorothy recalled hearing a crash, but admitted she did not investigate it. A short time afterward she thought she heard someone calling and went out to the top of the stairs with two other women who had left their rooms.

Looking down they saw Marval lying at the foot of the stairs, with Stella crouched beside her. The injured woman was able to speak, and dismissed it all as a foolish accident, but a doctor was sent for anyway. Stella endeavoured to make her comfortable and to speak some reassuring words. She told her she would probably have to go to the hospital, but Marval laughed this off. A few minutes later she was dead.

An inquest determined that she died of a blood clot in the brain from the trauma of the fall. The attending physician, Joseph Gibbs, was satisfied that there were no suspicious injuries and her death was entirely accidental. A few days later the coroner, Edward C. Hart, and the jury, after hearing all the testimony, came to the same conclusion.[2]

It shocked Stella to see her friend, full of laughter and enthusiasm for her new business, suddenly lying lifeless and it strengthened her resolve to move ahead in her own life. Sympathetic, yet always on the lookout for opportunities, Stella took Vera aside and proposed that she take over the sale of the business that Marval had signed on December 4 for $4,200, giving her all "goods, chattels, personal property and effects." The first instalment of $300 was paid to Marval's estate, the remaining $3,900 to Vera Ashton until it was completely discharged on August 22, 1901.[3]

Stella was now the sole proprietress and tenant of the upper two floors of a three-storey building known as the Duck Block, after its owner, Simeon Duck. At that time Broad Street was a rough area and many small brothels existed on the two blocks between Yates and Pandora streets. Other nearby businesses nicely complemented the brothels. Within a one-block radius there were the Dixi Ross Company, suppliers of food and, more importantly, alcohol, the Eagle Bath and Barbershop, and a number of saloons including the Manhattan and the London Hotel. Next to Stella's place was the Lyceum Music Hall, formerly known as the Trilby.

The Lyceum was open from 8:00 PM to midnight all year round and advertised itself as "The Home of Mystery, Mirth, Amazement and Amusement"; it was affordable, with admission ranging from 10 to 25 cents. The theatres and music halls were where the madams could show their girls off. In fact, the police chief had arranged that a portion of the theatre be set aside for these women. That way they were easily identifiable to anyone who was interested, but not mixed with the respectable theatre-goers. This, as well as riding around in carriages, was the madams' primary mode of advertising.

Stella's first brothel in Victoria was on the top two floors of this building, the Duck Block. [CITY OF VICTORIA ARCHIVES CVA-96609-01-5789]

Around the corner on Government Street, the Delmonico Music Hall had similar seating arrangements.

Stella settled in well. The Duck Block was nicely decorated; it had a large parlour on the second floor for entertaining and several small rooms for the other activities, though the main private rooms were upstairs. Stella commissioned a photograph showing the main hall and two women she identified as Howard and Tusky. She also wrote on the back of the photograph "The fatal hall and stairs of Victoria, B.C., This is a hot time," as a bizarre memento of the tragic event that had taken place there. The photo does show the staircase between the second and third floors where Marval fell and also the entrance to the parlour on the left. It all looks like any respectable hotel; nothing indicates the nature of the business and even the women are sedately dressed in long, fashionable gowns.

Simeon Duck, Stella's landlord, was a well-known, long-time resident of the city and a colourful character. He arrived in Victoria in 1859, married in 1865 and opened a factory for the construction of wagons and carriages. He served in the legislature periodically throughout the 1870s and 1880s and was for a short time the Minister of Finance. What particularly stood out about Simeon Duck was his description of himself as a "free-thinker." Duck was renowned for his belief in the spirit world, a fashionable interest in the Edwardian period,

The interior of the Duck Block showing the staircase where Marval Conn fell to her death. [PRIVATE COLLECTION]

and his home was the scene of séances and meetings. In 1877 a reporter from the *Colonist* newspaper attended a series of séances at Duck's house and concluded that they were fraudulent.[4] Duck, however, was a true believer.

Apparently this free-thinking extended to a liberal attitude toward prostitution. Among the more sophisticated men about town it was considered quite acceptable as long as it operated discreetly. Being a businessman, Duck could appreciate the potential profits; the Duck Block had housed brothels for a number of years and Duck had not experienced any problems.[5] In fact, his prominence in the community afforded a form of protection for his tenant and her activities. Although the city officials were well aware of the problems in having what amounted to a red-light district in the city's centre, they did nothing about changing the situation until after Simeon Duck died in 1905.

Stella was enthusiastic about her new location and eager to put her experience to work in building the top parlour house in the city. There were already a few in Victoria, but they were small, plain and run very quietly. Stella would make a splash. With the knowledge she had gained in San Francisco, and the start Vera Ashton had made, she planned to put together an establishment that would outdo all others. It would be meticulously decorated and furnished, with an excellent selection of drinks, beautiful women and fine food available at any time.

She decided to operate on a boarding-house basis; the girls would rent a room in the brothel and keep their earnings while Stella would make money from food and liquor sales and the room rent. She started with four women, Dorothy Deane,

Maud Murphy, Hannah Johnston and Gladys Reilly, who ranged in age from 18 to 32. When the census taker came around in 1901, all of these women came up with legitimate professions—milliner, actress, dressmaker and typewriter— and reported their annual incomes as between $1,000 and $1,800. Stella claimed this amount too and gave her profession as "landlady."[6] It seemed like a reasonable amount, considering she knew that Police Chief John Langley made only $1,500 a year and in fact had just received a raise. She was fair and even generous to her "boarders" as long as they kept to her high standards, didn't try to usurp her role and stayed away from her men.

Her enthusiasm was high for another reason. She had a new lover. This was George A. Melbourne, occasionally known to authorities as George Montague. He had come up from Seattle with Stella and they were now living together in the brothel. He was a "bunco-man" or con artist and acted as a "mac," a combination of pimp, bouncer and Stella's man. They got along well and over the next five years they ran the brothel according to the custom of the local authorities. That is, they were subjected to a raid twice a year and paid the $50 to $100 fine, which was a sort of unofficial business licence. Otherwise, as long as there were no complaints and no trouble, they were left alone.

The police and the courts were not so charitable to George; they charged him as a "frequenter of a bawdy house" with a fine of $50 every time they found him in the brothel, even though they knew he was living with Stella. The police magistrate finally warned him that if he was caught again he would be given jail time. The next time he was to appear in court, in September 1905, he quietly left town and was out of Stella's life. She later discovered that he had written a farewell message in her old autograph book: "In your life's wreath of memory entwine one bud for me, Lovingly yours Geo. A. Melbourne."[7] She was quite broken-hearted and went around in a foul mood for some time, though madams of her stature and success did not stay alone for long. She even took her grief out on others.

That December she was charged with assaulting one of her girls, Teda Livingston, but the charge was dismissed when the complainant did not show in court. It had been a difficult year. Some months earlier Stella had been struck by a client, Frank Fredericks, in an argument over money and was rescued by George and her piano player, Hawky Dennis, who wrestled him to the ground and held him for the police.

Minnie was concerned about Stella's charges of assault as she, too, was familiar with her quick temper. She was certain that alcohol was playing a big part in her sister's problems and even sent her a comic postcard that proclaimed, "If Drinking interferes with your Business—Give up Business." In a handwritten note she added, "Get wise kid! And get off the coyote wagon," southwest slang for the police van.[8]

Their grandfather, "Uncle Billy," had passed away in Missouri and as a clear indication of his disappointment in Ben and Dennis, left them only five dollars, bequeathing all his property to his wife, Araminta. This caused some drama and ill feeling in the family but it was sorted out when Araminta made sure the property would pass to Ben and

Dennis upon her death. Minnie kept in close touch with all her cousins, Dennis's children, but Stella stayed more aloof from the situation. She was stung when Minnie sent her a copy of Uncle Billy's obituary, lauding him as an upstanding citizen: "Would that we had no worse citizens in any county than 'Uncle Billy' Carroll has been, we would then have no need of courts, courthouses or jails."[9] The irony of this statement was not lost on either of them.

Stella even gave a fleeting thought to retiring from her business. Late in the year she sent a postcard, showing stacks of gold piled up on plates, to Minnie, with the message:

> Dear Siss—How does this look to you? Wish we had enough to retire on. Ha Ha E.C. Minn—you may get a few from your banker Someday. Hope on Dear heart.[10]

However, she decided to focus on her establishment and an old threat to her livelihood that was re-emerging on the horizon.

The moral-reform movement wasn't new, but it was rapidly gaining importance as a major issue in municipal politics in Victoria and elsewhere. Some of Victoria's religious leaders had established the Temperance and Moral Reform Association in 1890. They sent a delegation to city council to express their fear that "the social evil in the city ... has grown of late to alarming proportions ... and is doing incalculable harm to our youth of both sexes."[11] While their concerns were noted, not much in the way of action was taken. As time went on the proponents of this movement became steadily more organized and acquired the support of many prominent citizens. By the early 1900s other groups, such as the Voters'

League, Purity League, Women's Christian Temperance Union, Ministerial Association and Central Union of Christian Endeavour, grew more vocal in their frustration with what they viewed as political inaction against a society on the verge of moral deterioration.

By 1906 the reformers had heard enough vague promises and decided it was time for action; they were successful in electing one of their own, Alfred James Morley, as mayor on January 18. This was a hard-fought battle. Morley's adversary was a prominent funeral director, Charles Hayward, who counted among his supporters many of the established business and political elite.

The *Colonist* described Hayward as "an old and tried servant of the Corporation, representing the conservative business of the city and their aims and aspirations." Morley was characterized as a "radical of the pronounced type [who will bring his] half-baked, half-digested theories of municipal government into execution."[12] Despite his well-connected backers and the fact that he had already served three one-year terms as mayor from 1900 to 1902, Hayward was defeated. The electorate was obviously not worried about Morley's "theories" and he triumphed, receiving 1,429 votes to Hayward's 1,241 in a record turnout.[13]

The 44-year-old Morley, a mechanical engineer by trade, was a man of energy and vision who genuinely wanted to make Victoria a city everyone could be proud of, at least those of the right race and colour. He was an avid proponent of Asiatic exclusion and his racist views found favour with those who believed their livelihoods were threatened by an influx of "foreigners."

Victoria's "moral reform" mayor, Alfred J. Morley, circa 1906. He made private deals with Stella and then reneged on them.
[CITY OF VICTORIA ARCHIVES CVA-96604-01-2762]

He once stated, "Hindus were not wanted to mix with the people of this country."[14] He was the impetus behind many city improvements such as the Sooke Lake water system, the widening of streets, the installation of wood-block paving and the cluster lights, which are still a highly recognizable symbol of Victoria.

He was also noted for his commitment to the ideals of moral reform and lost no time in communicating the boundaries of his tolerance to the city at large. On January 25, 1906, the *Colonist* reported that police officials had visited saloon-keepers throughout the city to advise them that the Sunday closing by-law would from then on be strictly enforced. All saloons must close their doors and dismiss their customers by 11:00 PM on Saturday night and their premises must remain closed until 1:00 PM on Monday. Further, and more important to Stella, the police had received direct orders from Mayor Morley that no house of prostitution would be allowed to sell liquor at any time. These "new" regulations, which in fact had been on the books for some time, were said to be exciting "no end of talk among the sporting element, who fear that Victoria will be a 'closed town' for a year at least."[15] Certainly it was a major concern for Stella, who had envisioned a highly successful future with little interference from the authorities. Clearly that would not be the case.

Morley was already basking in the glow of congratulations from reformist and fraternal groups. The Emmanuel Baptist Congregation and the Centennial Methodist Church both announced in the newspapers that they did "hail with delight the attitude of Mayor Morley in the suppression of gambling and the control of other forms of vice."[16] For a man who had only been in office one week he had made an impression. It was clear that Morley would be death to any attempts to pervert the wholesome image of beautiful Victoria.

Back on Broad Street, Stella viewed this latest development with considerable dismay, and on the Sunday afternoon following the election she sat down to write a quick postcard to Minnie in Albuquerque:

Dear Siss: Back to the cactus with me—if matters don't change. Things did look good once & may again. E.C.[17]

In the end Stella decided the best strategy would be to keep a low profile and indulge in her other money-making interest, the buying and selling of real estate. According to an article in the *Colonist*, "Fine Outlook for Real Estate," it was a very good time to be doing this. Stella began negotiations for investment property while keeping an eye out for suitable premises in which to conduct her own business. One that interested her was the popular Goldstream Hotel, owned by Arthur Slater and James Phair. Stella had always been partial to a country life and the Goldstream Hotel was well situated; it was in a lovely rural area yet readily accessible by road and train. It was described as a going concern that "also embraces 30 acres of land, livestock, etc."[18] Stella bought a *lis pendens* (right to purchase), but Slater and Phair, for reasons unknown, tried to get out of this commitment. After much wrangling, Stella took the matter to the Supreme Court, which upheld her right to maintain the lis pendens but added the stipulation that she must put up $2,000 as security.[19] She declined to do this and the property eventually was sold to another party.

Stella carried on through the winter, even indulging in such mundane pursuits as spring-cleaning. She could have hired help and did occasionally have a housekeeper but the truth was she loved to maintain her own possessions, admiring each piece as she lovingly cleaned and polished. Few house-keepers could meet her high standards. She always made time for a quick excursion to shop or to visit friends in Vancouver or Seattle, or to attend the horse races. Racing was a happy diversion, a good place to parade her girls and to bet on the racehorse known as Estella—named for her by a loyal client. She was also arranging the sale of one of her properties in Winslow.

Morley, in the meantime, was beginning to ruffle feathers among his colleagues. In a February debate of estimates at a meeting of the school trustees, he accused the committee members of being discourteous, while Trustee Agnes Deans Cameron, herself no stranger to controversy, called Morley's comments insulting.[20] Soon he was clashing with other civic officials and aldermen, and it was becoming apparent that, while he was a man of determination and vision, he sorely lacked the qualities of tact and diplomacy.

As Stella and Morley continued to take care of business in their different ways, a distraction came with the frightful news of the earthquake in San Francisco on April 18, 1906. It was not the earthquake but the resulting fires that destroyed much of the Tenderloin district and forced many people out onto the streets, their possessions totally lost. It was a great social leveller too, as remarked on by a reporter for the *Oregonian* who wrote, "Painted women from the underworld ... and ladies, who, a week before, had ridden in their carriages, walk[ing] shoulder to shoulder, convers[ing] glibly. Caste and social standing were nothing."[21] Many of Stella's friends and colleagues were homeless, injured or even dead. Tessie Wall survived, although her house on Powell Street did not. However, Stella didn't have to worry, for a wealthy backer came to her rescue and Tessie was quickly back in business in a brand-new, three-storey, brick-and-terra-cotta building. It would play an important role in Stella's future.

For the San Francisco madams and brothel inmates it was time to move on, at least for a while, and many set their sights on cities up the coast, including Vancouver and Victoria. A few even looked up their old friend Stella and by June her business was booming. Things grew lively with the increased competition and Stella was again accused of assault, this time by a newcomer to the city, Alice Thorn, who thought she could challenge Stella's authority in her own house.[22] This charge was dismissed as Alice didn't appear in court and, presumably with Stella's blessings, moved on to another area.

In September Morley received what amounted to a report card on his work in cleaning up the city. The Citizens League held a public meeting with, as guest speaker, the Reverend Thomas William Gladstone, who reported that some improvement had been made in reducing the numbers of "those who live on the wages of immorality." He went on to warn that this would mean a decrease in profits for some who would not be recognized as partners but nevertheless profited from this traffic, a thinly veiled dig at property owners, investors and suppliers to the brothels. He also took the opportunity to remind his audience that campaigning for the municipal election would soon begin and citizens must let it be known that they stand for "cleanliness, clean methods, clean men, a clean city."[23]

In December the Local Council of Women passed a resolution asking provincial authorities for a "very careful police inspection of steamships running between neighbouring ports and Victoria," checking for incoming prostitutes. It was noted that, after much discussion with the "deepest of Christian feelings," the overall sentiment was one of heartfelt sympathy and a desire to help their fallen sisters.[24] There was in fact an interesting point of difference between the male view of moral reform—the casting out of the "social evil" and the protection of the young men of the town—and the female view—concern, and a wish to rescue the unfortunate women. As Stella didn't see herself as evil or unfortunate, the existence of these groups mattered to her only in terms of how much political influence they could exert.

For the moment, she was much too busy to worry about the dire rumblings. Her brother Roy had come up for a visit and the two were involved in legal transactions and real estate deals. In October they travelled to Vancouver, Seattle and Los Angeles, returning later that month. In November, Stella wrote Minnie that she would be going south again later and added excitedly that she had just sold a property in Victoria, which she had purchased three years previously, for $15,000.[25] She was still anxious to find a place of her own, but it was prudent to keep an eye on the upcoming civic election to see whom and what she might be up against in her efforts to maintain a viable trade.

Once again, moral reform emerged as an issue despite the best efforts of many citizens to downplay the problem. At a council meeting in early December, Morley introduced a bylaw amending the liquor-licence regulations. A heated debate ensued in which Alderman Alexander Stewart ventured his opinion that far too much was being said about the morality of the city and that Victoria was getting a lot of needless bad advertising. Morley quipped sarcastically, "Who is doing the advertising?" to which Stewart retorted, "You are doing considerable."[26] The bylaw was defeated, but the suggestion that Morley was perhaps making too much of the morality question was to linger into the pre-election debates.

All this intense wrangling was set aside, as such things always are, for the Christmas season. Social engagements were organized and the round of parties began. It was time to think of others less fortunate, and many people down on their luck were given extra food and comfort by the various charities that tried to ease their hunger and loneliness. Even the inmates of the provincial jail benefited from this generosity; they were treated to a special breakfast, lunch and dinner, largely through the efforts of the prison doctor, James D. Helmcken, who annually enlisted donations from others and gave a generous amount of fruit and candy himself.

This year the provisions included a "handsome donation from Miss Carroll of turkeys, fruit, etc."[27] Stella remembered all too vividly what it was like to do without and became as well known for her generosity, particularly to the inmates of the jail and to the children at the orphanage, as she was for her business activities. In 1908 her generosity was again mentioned in the newspaper: a donation by Miss E. Carroll of a pail of candy and a box of apples for the B.C. Protestant Orphans' Home.

In early January it was time for the annual civic election. Morley was running against Thomas Wilson Paterson, a Liberal and the president of the Board of Trade who was a private contractor for public works. Morley's supporters were branded Socialists, so-called moral reformers and people on the "outs with the existing conditions."[28] Morley himself was enthusiastically endorsed by *The People's Press*, a left-wing publication "Through Which the General Public May Express Their Thoughts Freely."

> The *Times* intimates that Mr. Morley is both dishonest and dishonorable. Such statements only act as a boomerang that will hit, not only the newspaper that makes them, but also the candidate in whose interests they are made. Doubtless, Mr. Patterson, [sic] as the *Times* states, is shrewd. Had he not been, he could not have collected his vast wealth from the earnings of his employees.[29]

Rallies and heated debates were held; accusations, denouncements and yelling matches entertained and amused the voting public. Morley did his best to keep moral reform an issue, and even Paterson's supporters admitted that he did deserve credit for his strict stance.

On the eve of the election the *Colonist*, which had come out in support of Paterson, tried to dissuade the public from making moral reform the point on which they would base their vote:

Just a word to those people, who have persuaded themselves that in some special way Mr. Morley's candidature is in the interest of moral reform. Such an idea has no solid basis. The cause of morality has not been advanced by so much as a hair's breadth by reason of the incumbency of the civic chair by Mr. Morley ... The vicious element in the town have never ... been in control of city matters ... there is no issue of morality in the pending election for the mayoralty.[30]

Morley triumphed. During the evening of Election Day, January 17, crowds gathered outside City Hall as the count was carried out. Ironically, considering that the moral-reform issue covered gambling as well, men moved through the crowds taking bets on the outcome. Finally at 9:30 PM the results were announced and the crowd erupted in cheers for a speech by the returned mayor. As he stated, it was not a fight for Morley, but a fight for principle, and principle had won. For Stella it was just another obstacle in her path to a successful and profitable business. Once again she would lie low and wait to see what the indefatigable Morley would do.

This time Morley didn't leap in quite as quickly as he had the previous year; he took time to consider some alternatives for dealing with the brothel situation. Of the established "carriage house" madams, Alice Seymour, Jennie Morris and Fay Watson owned houses at the south end of the city's core. They catered to, among others, the members of the Union Club, a private men's establishment patronized by many of the city's influential businessmen. They rarely appeared in the newspapers and it was understood that they were well protected. All of the other madams who had rented premises on Broad Street had moved on, with one very notable exception: Stella. It was essential that she be moved out of the area as well, to complete the illusion that there had been a thorough cleanup. This was merely for show, of course, as most of the women had simply relocated farther north, to Chatham and Herald streets, which had quietly been designated the unofficial "restricted district."

On March 1 the Board of Police Commissioners instructed Police Chief John Langley to inform the occupant, that is, Stella, of 60½ Broad Street (the Duck Block) to vacate and to take all necessary measures to achieve this. The next day Langley was on Stella's doorstep informing her of this development. Stella immediately wrote to Minnie:

> Dear Siss: Just rec'd official notice that we are all to Move—very
> shortly Very unsettled. Expect to know more tomorrow.
> With love Siss EC[31]

What took place the next day, at a secret meeting of Stella, Mayor Morley and Chief Langley, was to become the subject of legal debate for many months. Stella's lawyer, Tod Aikman, later claimed that Morley told Stella if she were to locate in the Herald Street area she would be permitted to operate unmolested. Morley declared that he had said nothing of the kind and that it was Chief Langley who had led Stella to think this. Whatever the case, Stella genuinely believed that if she cooperated, she would be left alone.

She visited the mayor at his office and in his words

Victoria Police Chief John Mount Langley, who found himself constantly caught between politics, the law and the reality of the demi-monde.

"begged" to be allowed to operate at the Duck Block for the remainder of the year. Morley stated that after consultation with Chief Langley, and taking into consideration unnamed others who had used their influence, Stella was given an extension of two months. Fortunately for her, some properties that would suit her quite well had come on the market; they were on Herald and Chatham streets, where she thought she might build her own house. Stella was highly distrustful of Morley but believed that a move to the restricted district would solve the problem. She would own her establishment and Morley would benefit from the appearance of having cleaned up the city. Besides, the only alternative was to leave town and she wasn't ready to do that yet.

Early in 1907 she purchased two lots from a pioneer lumberman, J. A. Sayward, and another one from the B.C. Land and Investment Company. These were all vacant lots in the 500 blocks of both Herald and Chatham. Unknown to Stella, a prominent businessman, Biggerstaff Wilson, who wished to build a cold-storage facility, coveted these same lots. Wilson was determined to have the property and worked out a deal to help Stella finance her purchase of other lots for her brothel.[32] On April 25 she bought two lots farther up Herald Street from a Chinese businessman, Yee Pack. One of these was unimproved but the other had a fine brick house which had been built for a brewer, Thomas Watson Carter, and had recently been the residence of Dr. Frank Hall. This house could provide her with the better class of operation she had longed for.

Not one to hesitate, Stella immediately hired an architect

Stella's house at 643 Herald Street as it looked in 1960. Its address was so notorious that when the house was sold for taxes in 1920, the numbers were changed to 679. The building still stands and has been, among other things, a bed-and-breakfast.
[CITY OF VICTORIA ARCHIVES CVA-98202-19]

and took out a building permit for extensive renovations. In short order she was changing a four-bedroom house into a brothel with living quarters for herself, dining and lounge areas, 12 small bedrooms and additional bathrooms. This was all expensive, of course, but she was confident that her business was now secure and her investment would be profitable over the long term.

However, on May 13 Chief Langley issued a bulletin to his men:

Having ussued [sic] all orders for the closing of the premises of "Stella Carrol" [sic] situated at 60½ Broad Street, Victoria, the same taking effect May 15, 1907, you are hereby ordered that if you find prsotitution [sic] going on in said pemises [sic] after that date, the offenders must be summoned to appear in Court for frequenting such place.[33]

While work continued on the Herald Street house, Stella decided to invest in a revenue-generating property nearby. On June 10 she bought a house on Chatham Street between Government and Douglas from Auguste Borde, the city's water collector. She rented the 1½-storey, wood-frame cottage to Maude Moore, who carried on a small-scale brothel operation. It was conveniently located adjacent to the bottling plant of the Victoria Phoenix Brewing Company, for easy access to both liquor supplies and brewery workers as clients. She financed this purchase through a $1,400 mortgage at 6 percent from Louisa Hall, a local woman. It was a short-lived investment for on July 23, a fire swept through this part of town and like many of the other buildings, the cottage was totally destroyed. Maude Moore and any visitors apparently escaped without injury.

The fire reportedly started in a disused boiler house near the Albion Iron Works at Store Street and Herald at about 2:30 PM. Strong winds and dry conditions in a very short time fanned a small blaze into a major conflagration that quickly spread along Chatham and Herald streets, lined largely by small frame shacks and cottages. Because these houses were part of the newly designated restricted district, prostitutes occupied most of them. The newspaper reported eyewitness accounts of terror-stricken, scantily clad women running into the streets, imploring aid to save their "meager belongings." One woman was said to have told onlookers she had been burned out in San Francisco after the great earthquake and that this "second visitation by fire was undoubtedly a visitation by Providence, and amid her heartbroken sobs, which left no doubt of her sincerity, declared her intention of hereafter leading an upright life."[34]

As the flames leaped from street to street, other residential areas were destroyed and it took several hours to get the fire under control. In all, more than 90 buildings were destroyed and over 250 people made homeless. Police Chief Langley was asked what steps would be taken now that the restricted district had been destroyed. He replied:

> The women will have to leave town unless they can at once secure new homes in the district they have just left. We do not intend to take any harsh measures unless forced to and we shall give them reasonable time to make their arrangements, but they will not be permitted to scatter permanently among the uptown hotels and lodging houses. Chatham Street is the only place where they can be tolerated and that is wiped out. The result is that they will have to go.[35]

His statement made no sense at all. First he said they had to leave, and then that they could stay if they could find a place to live on Chatham (there was no mention of Herald

Street—obviously that was too sensitive) but they could not move anywhere else. Despite the chief's declaration, the women dispersed to hotels and lodging houses and then rebuilt on Chatham and Herald, or simply waited until others did and moved back. A few left town but others quickly arrived to take their place.

The newspapers printed the street addresses and lot numbers of the properties that had sustained losses along with the names of the property owners. It was interesting for people to see exactly who was profiting from the excessive rents in the restricted district. Many owners listed were Chinese but it was rumoured that they were agents for others who wished to be anonymous.

Fortunately for Stella, who had moved all her belongings in on May 1, her main house on Herald Street was untouched. She delayed starting up her business, though, as she and Roy went to southern California to spend the Fourth of July with their father, Ben, and his family.

The ever-generous Stella lavished attention, in the form of presents and brand-new outfits, on her young half siblings, Beatrice, William and John, and declared them "cute and smart." They had a family postcard taken in front of a seaside backdrop, with Stella looking elegant and confident in contrast to her father's beautiful young Cherokee wife, Mattie, and her three children, who appeared a bit dubious about the whole affair. Stella sent a copy to Minnie with a pencilled note: "Whole D[amn] family July 4, 1907."[36]

The following week she and Roy returned to Victoria, to witness the devastation caused by the fire. The loss of the

Stella, Roy, Ben and his wife Mattie and their three children, Beatrice, John and William— "Whole D[amn] Family, July 4, 1907." Stella couldn't resist dressing everyone up to have their picture taken.
[PRIVATE COLLECTION]

Chatham Street house was a shock but Stella, having learned her lessons from previous disasters, was insured for $500 and rebuilt her house, again renting out to one of her displaced colleagues.

Now established on Herald Street she opened for business and was settling in to what she believed, due to the assurances of the mayor, would be a smooth tenure with few disruptions. She operated with as few as two girls during the week, or as many as nine on the weekends. She had her piano for additional entertainment and Quong, her cook, would supply a meal if required. She still operated as a boarding-house establishment, which left her free to travel because the house could operate under the care of one of the girls. Even her lawyer, Tod Aikman, took time to go to Seattle, where he married his current companion, a widow with three young children.

Life was proceeding quietly until November 29, when Chief Langley issued another bulletin:

INSTRUCTION TO MEMBERS OF THE POLICE DEPT.—
Stella Carrol [*sic*] who occupied the Duck Block on Broad Street is now living at 643 Herald Street, usually

Police mug shots of Lizzie Cook and Martha Roberts, two of the girls who worked for Stella at her Herald Street brothel. [VICTORIA POLICE MUSEUM AND ARCHIVES]

known as Dr. Frank Hall's house. It has been reported to me that this is being or about to be used as a house of prostitution. Sergeants therefore must instruct their constables to keep a strict watch in this matter. Should they find any evidence of such prostitution send in [the word "arrest" is crossed out] the inmates forthwith.[37]

This was an unexpected move on the chief's part, a surprise even to members of the force but not to Stella. Chief Langley and Mayor Morley were both aware that she had purchased the property earlier in the year and was renovating it for one clear purpose. It was they who had delineated the restricted district and told her that she would have to move from Broad Street to Chatham or Herald. It was also they who had given her an extension on her time in the Duck Block until she found other premises.

Why the sudden crackdown? Stella hoped it was all idle threats but as she thought back, the signs were all there. She had heard that Morley had been snooping around her place, asking questions about the renovations. She also knew some neighbours had been complaining and that the reform groups had been watching her house for signs of operation. More important, after she had purchased the property and begun renovations she was asked to meet with Morley and Langley again.

This time the meeting was not about moving to the restricted district, which she had done, but an attempt to dissuade her from opening. Needless to say, this did not sit well with Stella, who had poured a lot of money into redoing the building. She was outraged by what she saw as their reneging on their previous agreement, and saw her hopes of a quiet, profitable life fading. She had faithfully kept her part of the bargain and spent much of her capital doing so; then they had betrayed her. It was not fair.

Morley and the chief suggested she might try operating it as a boarding house, a ridiculous suggestion considering the difference in potential profits. As voices were raised and the staff at City Hall strained to hear the exchange in the mayor's office, the meeting ended abruptly; Stella stormed out, yelling her vow to run despite them all. It was clear that the battle lines had been drawn. Determined though the mayor and chief were to take back their assurances that she could run unmolested, they were about to find out that the indomitable Stella Carroll could be just as stubborn.

five

Remember Me is All I Ask,

       But if Rememberance [sic] Proves a Task, Forget

I T SEEMED HARD TO BELIEVE but a whole year had gone by, and after the Christmas celebrations, the 1908 municipal election was upon them. This New Year heralded a promising start for Stella: Alfred Morley was defeated by a dentist and incumbent alderman, Lewis Hall. In late December, at a meeting of the Citizens League, Morley declared himself a friend of moral reform, even going so far as to mention that a house lately opened up on Herald Street "which has recently been fitted up, was being watched by police with the object in view of securing a conviction against it of being a disorderly house."[1] Once again, Stella's place was to be used as Morley's "issue."

His adversary, Hall, countered Morley with his own solemn

promise to continue the work in moral reform. He then went one better by announcing that some years before, he had taken the pledge of the Good Templars and was a total abstainer from alcohol. Morley admitted that he sometimes took a glass of ale or wine but was committed to the cause anyway.

Another attack on Morley came during a council meeting when Alderman Hanna accused him of telling indecent and vulgar stories in committee meetings. Morley's only reply to Alderman Hanna was, "Shut up."[2] Morley's poor record in dealing with his colleagues, while amusing, did point out the very real dilemma that little was being accomplished in this atmosphere of hostility and personal attacks. Morley accepted his defeat with equanimity, but was sure that some day he would be back. Others thought this quite possible too and were determined to head off any chance of his return.

Stella was glad to see the end of Morley. Late in his campaign he had boasted of having closed down the brothels on Broad Street and had gone on to claim victory in closing the establishments of other madams elsewhere in the city core. This was not true.[3] Alice Seymour ran her house at 715 Broughton Street until 1915, Jennie Morris was at 621 Courtney Street until 1912, and Fay Watson at 824 Douglas Street until at least 1909. Unlike Stella, these women were rarely brought into court. Their houses were quiet and catered to the affluent.

Stella did not wish to have the political spotlight constantly aimed on her and the whole moral-reform question. She was anxious to get down to business and, provided Chief Langley stayed out of the way, she intended to do just that. She knew she would have to hold her temper; getting into fights with the girls or worse, the customers, was drawing too much attention. With Morley out of the way, Stella was confident that if she ran a low-key house, Langley would back off. The damage had been done, though, and Stella was just too well known for the police to overlook her activity. Besides, Langley was wary of the city's politicians and the police commission. He knew he could well be made the scapegoat if the public continued to press for moral reform.

By late January things in Victoria were hopping. Many dignitaries, visitors and journalists were in town for the grand opening of the Canadian Pacific Railway's newest hotel, The Empress, and this meant steady business for Stella. Around midnight on the evening of January 21, 1908, a handsome, dark-haired, blue-eyed, well-dressed man by the name of Fred C. Brewer arrived at Stella's. He was in a hired car, with a group of friends in a partying mood. Identifying himself as a journalist in town for the opening of The Empress, he explained that he had unfortunately run short of cash and asked if Stella would pay the driver the $10 owing and add it to the considerable tab he planned on running up at her place. Against her better judgment (she could always be swayed by dark hair and blue eyes), she decided to take a chance, paid the driver and admitted the boisterous group.

In all, the party consumed 14 bottles of champagne in addition to the drinks on the house proffered by Stella and her housekeeper, Therese Roberts. The cost of the alcohol was $75, and additional unspecified goods or services were $65. At the end of the evening Brewer asked Stella for a blank cheque from the Northern Bank, which he had Therese fill out in the amount of $150; he signed and his group departed. When the cheque was handed in to the Northern Bank the next day it was found to be worthless, as Brewer did not have an account with them.[4] Stella's sense of fair play was offended again; infuriated, she headed to the police station to lay a complaint. Brewer was picked up the same day, his "mug shot" taken and his particulars recorded. According to the information he gave, he was actually a marine engineer.[5]

In his initial court appearance Brewer described his actions as a foolish escapade. He claimed that he had arrived in town five or six weeks earlier to conduct some unspecified business. While partaking of lunch in a local restaurant he happened to overhear that a number of CPR officials and their guests were in one of the private boxes, and managed to include himself by convincing them he was a journalist from Winnipeg. Established as an invited member of the press, Brewer headed over to The Empress to enjoy a lavish dinner and a good deal of wine, which he charged to his room. He booked one of the cars reserved for official guests and, with a group of friends, spent the evening driving and partying around town, eventually ending up at Stella's. Brewer's efforts to establish this as a trivial antic did not sit well with the magistrate who remarked it was a serious matter; Brewer was charged with obtaining goods under false pretences. It was a triumph for Stella, but a hollow one, as she in turn was charged with keeping a disorderly house. The cases were to be tried together.[6]

When the cases came before the court, the cheque was submitted in evidence and the bank clerk questioned. Brewer

Fred C. Brewer was a con man who got away with passing a bad cheque at Stella's Herald Street house, despite her having had him prosecuted. To him, it was merely a foolish escapade. [VICTORIA POLICE MUSEUM AND ARCHIVES]

claimed that he had not received value for his money. No defence witnesses were called. His lawyer, Richard C. Lowe, argued that nowhere was the testimony clear on whether the wine had been given for the promise of a cheque. The presiding judge, Peter Lampman, concurred, stating that Brewer never did say which bank the cheque would be drawn on nor that he had funds there. Brewer was acquitted. Stella, however, was convicted and fined $50. The loss of the $150, combined with the fine, made the total cost of this futile exercise $200, plus a great deal of aggravation. To make matters worse, two of her girls, Pearl Vise and Blanche Marguerite, were convicted with her and fined $25 each.[7]

Though she was driven by justifiable outrage at being cheated, it was an ill-thought-out move on Stella's part to bring herself to the attention of the authorities, and it was made worse because the story of Brewer's escapade was widely recorded in the newspapers. The illusion that the brothels had been shut down was shattered. Private citizens, such as Mrs. Hastings, who lived one block up from Stella, were furious.[8] Sylvestria Theodora Hastings was a force to be reckoned with. She was a suffragette who is said to have been the first woman to vote in a municipal election in British Columbia. She put her complaints about Stella in a letter to the city council, which referred it to the Health and Morals Committee. In the past, Sylvestria had tried talking to both the former mayor, Morley, and Chief Langley but to no avail. They were probably worried that the assurances they had given in their private meetings with Stella would be revealed. They were right to be concerned.

The committee agreed that Stella's house should not have been allowed to open; indeed, from the information its members received, they believed that the owner had been warned of this. They were not made aware that originally Stella had been told she could operate on Herald Street so they had no alternative but to ask the police to shut her down.[9] Following orders, the police raided her place regularly, even bringing in a hired detective from Vancouver to work undercover. This was becoming a common practice; detectives from agencies such as Thiel's and Pinkerton's were often called upon to pose as customers and gather evidence on the sale of liquor and the character of the house. It was proving effective and after several convictions for keeping a bawdy house and selling liquor without a licence, Stella and her lawyer, Tod Aikman, decided to initiate an all-out attack on what they perceived as her persecution.

At Stella's March appearance (she was now in court on a regular basis, once a month), their first retaliation was launched. Stella was charged with keeping a bawdy house and the prosecutor, Langley, called Constable Heather to the stand. As reported in the *Times*:

> No sooner had the good Heather taken his seat ... and settled himself down to tell the court the story of his visit to the palace of Miss Carroll than Mr. J.A. Aikman interposed with the fatal words "I object."[10]

It was a long afternoon of points of law and legal debate, the main objection being that Heather had not, by his own admission, given the required statutory warning and therefore the evidence of the police officers who had been conducting surveillance on the house was inadmissible. Despite this, the court was told that three or four respectable men had been seen to enter the house and one intoxicated man had been refused admittance. Aikman argued that this could be seen at any hotel or private house in the city and proved nothing. Magistrate Jay, clearly worn down by the abstruse arguments, rendered his judgment that the charge had been proved and that besides, Miss Carroll had been convicted of the same charge the previous month. No sooner were these words out of his mouth than Aikman was on his feet once more.

Police Magistrate George Jay, who saw nearly as much of Stella as her customers did.
[BC ARCHIVES G-1348]

"I object. I would point out to Your Honour that you cannot consider the previous convictions," said Mr. Aikman.

"Oh yes I can," said Mr. Jay.

"Oh no you can't," said Mr. Aikman."[11]

And on it went until Jay handed down the $90 fine, payable within five days. Aikman retaliated with his intention to appeal and then added for no apparent reason the fact that his client, Stella Carroll, was worth between $12,000 and $15,000. The magistrate's only reply was, "Next case."[12]

Stella was content to leave the legal affairs in Aikman's capable hands because she had other, more personal, matters on her mind. Just two days after the decision was handed down, she left for San Diego, California. She sent a cryptic postcard to her sister indicating that she was attempting a visit with their father, Ben, whose drinking was out of control:

> Dear Siss: Arrived here the 2nd found things bad as could be. Old Gent sick at San Diego. Children well. Establ. is bar room. Write soon EHC [13]

Five days later she was in Los Angeles with her brother Roy and wishing that Minnie could be there too. She would have liked to regale them with tales of her legal battles in Victoria with her reliable lawyer, Aikman. In her business there were few she could trust, and this made her family all the more important. She didn't have to hide anything from them.

As summer approached Stella was back in Victoria and open for business, though Langley was just waiting for the opportunity to close her down. On June 15 she was once again brought up on charges of keeping a disorderly house for which she was fined $50. A second charge for selling liquor without a licence was heard on June 27. These charges were laid through the efforts of undercover detectives William Wadman and Allen de Taube from Vancouver, who had visited Stella's house on several occasions. They both testified to having bought drinks directly from Stella and her houseboy-cum-cook, Quong, as well as accepting several rounds of free drinks from the ever-generous Stella. Aikman argued that despite this testimony, it had not been proven that Stella was the proprietress or even an occupant of the house and that if she accepted money, it was only a necessary evil that anyone would accept.[14] It was certainly common knowledge in the court that Stella owned the building and had been prosecuted and convicted many times, yet Aikman's tactics seemed to work.

He was a shrewd and effective lawyer who used whatever means he could to secure an acquittal for his clients. The 36-year-old Aikman had been practising since 1893 in the Kootenays and the Yukon, as well as Victoria. He had recently married, although his wife suffered from depression, and with three young stepchildren life may have been challenging for someone not used to the role of family man. Well connected—his father had been a King's Counsel—Aikman was founder and later president of the McBride Conservative Club and had a lifelong commitment to the Conservative Party both provincially and federally. Stella had learned from him and followed his advice, with success, so it did not take much persuasion for her to agree to expose the manoeuvrings of the past. For Aikman it was a way to ensure that former mayor Morley's political future (it was widely believed he would run again) would be extinguished and the political interests of the conservative business elite of the city preserved.

Aikman's defence was to point out that both Morley and Langley (with emphasis on Morley) knew all about Stella's business. He further charged that in an effort to appear to be cleaning up the city, the mayor and chief had only relocated the houses of prostitution to the unofficial restricted district, Herald and Chatham streets. Aikman alleged that Stella was the scapegoat for all of the more discreet operators in the city, that she was being persecuted while others ran openly. With his "cards on the table" stance, he admitted that, yes, it was against the law to run a house of prostitution, but his client's place was no worse than the others; in fact, it was conducted in a much better way and it was "not British fair play to harass his client."[15] He then made public what had been known on the streets for months: that Morley, in his desperation to get Stella out of the Duck Block and off Broad Street, had told her that if she went to Herald Street she would not be harassed. She had bought the property, invested $15,000 in renovations and moved in two weeks earlier than the deadline to vacate the Duck Block. She had done exactly what they asked, but now the rules had changed.

Next up was Police Chief Langley who stated that he resented the allegation that he was persecuting the woman and that he was bound to act on the instruction of the police board, whose chair in 1906 had been Mayor Morley. In other words, it was all Morley's fault. This revelation was hot copy, particularly for the *Times*, whose front-page headline that same evening read:

SAYS EX-MAYOR GAVE AUTHORITY—STARTLING STATE-MENT IN THE CARROLL CASE—Council [*sic*] for Defense Announces Client Was Told to Locate on Herald Street[16]

Morley wasted no time in getting a letter to the paper explaining his side of the story. He unequivocally denied that he had given any such assurances; to the contrary, he had repeatedly told Stella she would not be permitted to open. He claimed that Stella had told him Langley had given these assurances, but of course Langley denied this. Morley then reflected back to the "secret" meeting held in his office in early 1907, when they both attempted to convince Stella that a well-run boarding house might be a good business in that location. The ex-mayor recollected that, after a full 30 minutes of arguing, cajoling and threats on all sides, Stella had departed the office with a flourish, declaring she would run the house in spite of them. He then expressed surprise and disappointment that her house had been allowed to run wide open for nearly half a year, the intimation being that Mayor Hall, the Police Board and Chief Langley were not doing their duty.[17]

Despite all this controversy, Stella was again convicted. Aikman was true to his word and filed for a writ of certiorari with the Supreme Court of British Columbia. His case was based on the argument that it had not been proven that Stella had knowledge of unlawful acts being committed on her premises, while G. H. Barnard, KC, appearing on behalf of Magistrate George Jay, gave the police's evidence as to the reputation of the house. Chief Justice Gordon Hunter, who was presiding, felt it was important that the case be proven in a proper legal way, not just on reputation, and he quashed the conviction for keeping a disorderly house. This became the new tactic for dealing with Stella's convictions and was to prove successful in subsequent cases.[18]

Victoria City Council was disturbed because the judgment set a precedent and would make prosecuting any person for keeping a disorderly house futile. The ruling created quite a furor in legal circles and it was felt that the police would probably have to give up any attempts at securing convictions because they would be overturned on appeal. Accordingly, the council instructed the city's solicitor to request that Attorney General William Bowser appeal Chief Justice Hunter's decision. Bowser, who was known to oppose the prosecution and incarceration of prostitutes, declined, saying that if the city wished to appeal the case it could use the name of the attorney general but would have to bear all court costs. If the city chose not to continue, the only alternative was to change the law.[19]

For now, Stella was home free and she knew it. With political annoyances out of the way, her life entered a period of relative calm. She continued to follow her moneymaking pursuits—running her brothel on Herald Street and investing in real estate. She still had not achieved her dream: a truly upscale house with fine furnishings and an impressive and comfortable parlour where men could spend the entire evening listening to music and enjoying high-quality food

Attorney General William Bowser (later premier of British Columbia) stirred up controversy by ordering the release of women convicted of prostitution offences.

[BC ARCHIVES, C-00590]

and champagne, and then choose a companion with whom to spend the rest of the night. Discreet and elegant was what she wanted, and Herald Street just wasn't working out that way.

Once again Stella decided to look for a property in the country and in September 1908 she turned her attention to the municipality of Saanich, just outside Victoria. A popular establishment known as the Victoria Gardens Hotel was for sale; it was on The Gorge, a popular amusement area with an opera house, an outdoor moving-picture theatre, a dance pavilion and a Japanese tea garden.

Stella longed to have a grand "resort" and the Victoria Gardens Hotel, adjacent to the tramway, seemed to fit the bill. Two men who were to become her partners, Joseph H. Brown and William "Scotty" Paterson, purchased the hotel. Stella may have had a financial interest in this property, although it was prudent to keep this quiet for the time being, and she also bought a lot across the street.

But another property in the area had excited her interest: the Loewen estate, across from the Victoria Gardens Hotel, had just come on the market. It comprised 12 acres and was graced with a handsome and commodious Queen Anne-style house known as Rockwood, built for pioneer brewer Joseph Loewen in 1892. He had died in 1903 and his widow had now put the house up for sale.

This seemed an excellent idea to Stella because a portion of her business would be out of Victoria. The municipal election for January 1910 was on the horizon and Stella's old nemesis, Alfred Morley, was making a comeback. This way she would still have Herald Street, but if the heat became too intense she could always transfer her entire operation to the suburbs.

With Brown and Paterson, Stella purchased Rockwood.[20] Finally, she had what she had been looking for and she immediately set about redecorating, one of her favourite pastimes. The antiques and treasures she had acquired in Europe were installed, the walls were covered in fine wallpapers, lace and velvet curtains were hung, oriental carpets were laid, and expensive, leather-upholstered furniture brought in. A classical nude statue, a phonograph and even a stately portrait of herself were added. The rooms sparkled with finely polished silver and delicate crystal, and beautifully designed lamps cast their spell. When it was all done she commissioned a Victoria photographer, John Savannah, to record her achievement by taking pictures of some of the rooms as well as portraits of herself and even her five dogs. This was to be her home and her premier parlour house, for exclusive guests and private parties only.

Music filled the rooms on weekends and special occasions, when she brought in local and travelling musicians. Her favourite was a young piano player named Freddy Cole, a slight man of 21 years with dark brown wavy hair and blue eyes. He had more conventional jobs, as a taxi driver and a photo engraver with the *Times* newspaper, but his real love was music. Freddy craved a life of excitement; he drove too fast (on several occasions he was fined for driving over the 10-mile-an-hour speed limit), drank too much and frequented the opium dens in Chinatown. He loved the songs popular in the vaudeville theatres, such as "Cuddle Up A Little Closer, Lovey Mine" and "Oh! You Beautiful Doll."

They were standards in the brothels and reinforced the notion of women as cute little playthings, there expressly for the entertainment of the paying male customer. Some songs such as "In My Merry Oldsmobile" had lyrics that could be interpreted in a risqué fashion when sung with the right emphasis and a leering expression. "He'd have to get under— get out and get under ... [to fix up his automobile]." Other brothel songs were more to the point:

Are you gonna put it there, put it there?
Are you gonna put it there, put it there?
Come across you dirty louse—
This's a fifteen dollar house
If you're gonna put it there, pay your fare![21]

Parodies of current songs, with "dirty" lyrics, were popular for drunken singalongs. The music varied from house to house, but whatever the song, the musicians were well rewarded as the visitors attempted to outdo each other, proving their affluence by tipping generously. For Freddy it was a wonderful way to spend the weekend.

Quong, the Chinese cook, was in attendance here and occasionally at Herald Street to prepare meals as required. He met Stella's high standards and worked for her for several years. On more than one occasion he was arrested during a raid, an occupational hazard for any employee of a brothel, but it was understood that any bail or fine would be taken care of. Stella kept a larder of meat and game—Roy supplied her with fresh ducks from his hunting—and a full complement of the finest spirits and champagne, as well as wine and beer.

One of the greatest annoyances for a madam in Victoria and the outlying areas, like Saanich, was the constant threat of conviction for dispensing liquor without a licence. Brothels were strictly prohibited from possessing liquor licences (Minnie in Albuquerque didn't have this problem; there, houses of prostitution could be licensed). Liquor fines were higher than those for running a brothel, so Stella and her partners attempted to legalize this element of their business by applying for a licence. They were all aware that the name Stella Carroll was far too well known to be on the application so they decided to submit it under Scotty Paterson's name. He was a well-respected saloonkeeper in Victoria and it wasn't a new application; it was merely a request to transfer the Victoria Gardens Hotel licence to Rockwood:

> NOTICE—I hereby give notice that I will apply at the next sitting of the Board of License Commissioners of Saanich for a transfer of the license known as the Victoria Gardens Hotel to the house known as Rockwood on Gorge Road.
>
> (SIGNED) W. Paterson November 8, 1909[22]

For a while it seemed that the trio might pull off their scheme to obtain a liquor licence for a brothel, but their hopes were dashed, thanks to the *Times*. As required, Paterson had advertised his intention, carefully choosing to do this in the *Colonist* rather than the *Times*. Newspapers do keep a close eye on the competition, however, and the editor at the *Times* made sure that what was going on was soon common knowledge. "ROCKWOOD RESIDENCE TO BE ROADHOUSE," read the headline:

The property known as Rockwood, mentioned in the Advertisement, was formerly the Loewen homestead. It ... very recently was acquired by the person signing the ... advertisement and Miss Stella Carroll.

Residents along the Gorge road and in that section of the city generally do not view with favour this proposal to turn a fine old homestead, situated in the heart of a growing residential district, into a common road house, and rumours are afloat that a petition will be presented to the board of licensing commissioners praying that the application may not be granted.

It is felt that a saloon, as conducted by the persons who have acquired the property, would hardly enhance that section of the city as a desirable place of residence.[23]

The game was up and the application denied. Stella bought out Paterson and Brown's share of Rockwood and carried on, dispensing liquor without a licence as she had done before. She continued running Herald Street too, but she would have to be discreet: once again Morley had been elected mayor.

However, business matters were less of a concern at the moment; Stella was in love again. In July 1909 she had met and fallen for the bartender from the Vernon Saloon on Douglas Street, not far from her Herald Street brothel. It was always useful for madams to know bartenders, as they were helpful in directing out-of-town clients. Peter Jensen was handsome, with light brown hair, blue eyes and a charming Danish accent. He was a year older than Stella and a delightful companion in many respects. Unfortunately, like her first husband Dudley Curtis, he had a violent temper, which he took out on Stella on several occasions.

For all Stella's intelligence, strength and independence, this was the one aspect of her life in which she made bad decisions. Having lived from the time of her early teens without a mother, and with a father who was rarely around, Stella had never had good role models in her life. Despite an aloof exterior, she was a passionate woman and when she gave her heart, she did so completely. She always felt she could fix any situation in time, perhaps from having been the head of a family when she herself was very young, and she did not want to spend her life alone. She chose to put up with Peter's ill-treatment until an incident in August 1909 when she had him arrested and actually followed through by giving evidence to secure his conviction.

She had laid complaints before but usually retracted them. This time, with the support of Minnie, who was there on one of her frequent visits and had seen Peter's brutal attack at the Herald Street house, she testified against him along with Minnie and Constable Florence, who was also a witness. Ironically, the defence lawyer was Aikman.[24] Peter was fined $20. Stella promptly paid the fine and took the contrite man back, but was soon to learn the hard way that she was making a terrible mistake. For the time being, though, they would stay together and try to return to a more peaceful existence.

six

A Way Back Here and Out of Sight

I'll Write My Name Just For Spite

STELLA'S ATTEMPT AT LIVING a quieter life wasn't very successful. She was too well known. By 1910, moral reformers were again using all the influence they could muster to rid the city of "undesireables." And once again political foes were using this issue to uncover scandal and start smear campaigns. On March 14, 1910, the *Times* printed a letter attributed to "John Smith" which brought to light rumours which the writer felt should be investigated. These were mainly to do with Morley's function as mayor and called into question whether or not he was genuinely suppressing vice, that is, gambling and prostitution. The rumours contained hints of payoffs and kickbacks. As for Morley's "conservative" opponents, they were suspected of having powerful political influence over the appointments to the police commissioners board and the licence commissioners. The writer suggested that the provincial government should appoint a commission to investigate these rumours and that is just what the legislators did. They had little choice, as so much had been made of the allegations that it would have looked highly suspicious if they had not.

On March 23, 1910, the provincial executive endorsed a commission to be undertaken by Judge Peter Lampman to "make full enquiry into the official acts of the members of the Victoria Board of Police Commissioners for the present year."[1]

The commissioners who were being investigated were Alderman Harry Freake Bishop, Leonard Tait and the ever-controversial Mayor Alfred Morley.

More than 30 witnesses had been subpoenaed and the corridors were crowded with people of all social levels. Women of the demimonde lounged beside prominent business-men. Caucasian and Chinese gamblers sat alongside moral reformers, journalists and politicians.

Stella decided to stay far away from these proceedings. Aikman had advised that she keep a low profile and with his political connections, he would endeavour to keep her (and himself) off the list of people called to give testimony. In fact not many were summoned, save for the police commissioners themselves with their lawyers. Aside from this, the witnesses included a handful of police officers, moral reformers, professional gamblers and very few women of the demimonde.

Robert Dunn, editor of the *Times*, and William Blakemore, editor of *The Week*, claimed they had received much information from a variety of sources about the paying of "tribute" or protection money to preserve certain gambling establishments and houses of ill-fame from prosecution. They would not, however, reveal their sources. Eventually, testimony came around to who actually owned houses of ill-fame, how were they being managed and how it was that they were continuing to operate.

It was established that the houses on Chatham Street were owned by Chinese companies, with the exception of five duplexes built and owned by an Italian resident of North Vancouver, Lorenzo Reda. In subsequent testimony Reda admitted owning the houses but added that the land was leased from L. G. Quagliotti, a Victoria businessman. Both Reda and the Chinese companies were extracting exorbitant rents for the houses. Madams who rented them were interviewed and revealed that they were paying from $100 to $125 per month, with additional charges of $70 per month for furniture. Similar houses were being rented to "respectable people" for $15 per month. Reda maintained that he was merely a landlord, charging the going rate for a house in that neighbourhood, which of course was the restricted district that the police and politicians had unofficially set up some years earlier.

Stella held her breath when she read this in the newspaper but noted with some relief that no one was pointing a finger at her. She too still owned a house on Chatham Street which she rented to a "working girl," but no one seemed inclined to say that, even though the fact had been made public when the house was destroyed in the fire in 1907. She had rebuilt and, like Reda, was happy to rent it out for the high rates these properties garnered. She felt her place was much superior to anything the Chinese or Italian landlords had put up, and any tenant in the profession knew it was just the cost of doing business.

An unidentified working woman testified that she was certain two "up-town" houses of prostitution (probably Seymour's, Morris's or Watson's) must be paying some form of protection money or they would not be permitted outside the restricted district. She also said her attorney had informed her that she could receive protection through an Italian who owned the Chatham Street houses. She understood that this unnamed Italian was bribing police officials. It was pretty obvious to the court to whom she was referring. Oddly enough, though, no one seemed interested in the identity of the knowledgeable attorney, although to many that was obvious too. Tod Aikman was invariably the defence attorney for "sporting" women. William Lindley, a local furrier, testified that he had been told by his customers, who were also women of the demimonde, that they were having trouble with the police and that they were being "bled," having to pay so much money out to different interests.

Police Chief John Langley testified at length and was the only official who actually mentioned the name of Stella Carroll. Upon being questioned about the moral situation, he confessed that since the decision in the Carroll case, houses of ill-fame had not been interfered with to any extent. Like the police commissioners before him, he was asked why houses of prostitution outside the restricted district had not been closed and could only reiterate the explanation that because the madams owned them, they had decided to leave them alone for "the time being." Morley made the point that he had been against this decision, but Tait and Bishop had ignored him and directly instructed Langley to drop the case.

Langley also testified about how the police commissioners had set up the restricted district in 1907: the understanding was given the women that if they stayed in the area they would be left alone and for the most part they had been. Problems only arose when they tried to locate elsewhere. The chief went proudly on to record that during his career he had stopped the women from parading in the streets in open hacks and had set up restricted areas within the theatres.

There were numerous notable absences in this parade of characters. Aikman, Magistrate George Jay, madams Seymour, Watson and Morris, and Stella Carroll were never called, although they probably could have given much interesting evidence. As Stella read the testimony about houses owned by madams outside the restricted district being allowed to operate for "the time being," she had to wonder why her house, which she owned and was within the restricted district, was not. If that wasn't obvious persecution, she didn't know what else to call it. But discretion had become her new watchword. She would sit back with her feet up, pet dog in her lap and whisky in her hand, and watch the proceedings unfold through the journalistic eyes of the local newspapers. No doubt she had many a good laugh over the earnest statements and denials. She knew the truth, but she also knew better than to get involved.

As a wrap-up the Citizens League was allowed to have its say through its spokesman, Dr. Ernest Hall. A noted moral-reform speaker, Hall condemned the whole system of dealing

Stella followed the proceedings of the enquiry into the Victoria police commissioners from a discreet distance—her parlour at Rockwood. [PRIVATE COLLECTION]

with prostitution, stating that it would be best handled as a health issue, not a legal one.

"One bad woman in a community [is] worse than having bubonic plague, rabies, smallpox, scarlet fever and diphtheria together," he said.

"That's pretty bad," observed Judge Lampman.[2]

Lampman's final report concluded that the accusations against the commissioners were not well founded but did point out that there seemed to be a major inconsistency in their stance. They all were guilty of countenancing prostitution by the mere fact that they had set up a restricted district or allowed one to exist when keeping a common bawdy house was an offence under criminal law. However, he did agree that the justification was a valid one and constituted a policy precedent:

> In Victoria such houses have always been allowed, and in all other cities ... Everybody knows what these women are ... These women are too old to be reformed ... They cannot be imprisoned for the rest of their lives, and it would not be becoming for a Christian community to send them off to Seattle, Vancouver, or Nanaimo or some other neighbouring city. They are here now, have been here for years and we must keep them here, and the Commissioners have decided, wisely I think, that they do less harm where they are now ... So long as human nature is what it is today, the problem will remain.[3]

It had not gone unnoticed that by far the largest number of madams and prostitutes working the cities on the west coast, including Victoria, Vancouver and New Westminster, were American. Law-enforcement agencies and governments at all levels were finding their abilities to end or even control prostitution in the cities frustratingly futile. But there was a relatively easy solution to the "American" problem—deportation.

The federal government had already taken a lead role in this question. In 1907 Detective Edward Foster of the Dominion Police travelled to Vancouver and Victoria to ascertain just how widespread was the problem of American citizens, male or female, setting up houses of prostitution with American "inmates." After his three-month investigation Foster identified 80 prostitutes and madams in Vancouver who were American and they were ordered out of the city.[4] His work in Victoria is unknown but it was probably along the same lines. Canadian immigration authorities and police were pleased with Detective Foster's work, but noted that unless there were someone versed in police work to make systematic examinations of the restricted district, undesirables would continue to come in:

> Spasmodic clearing up at long intervals is of no use and already I believe some of the houses of ill-fame have commenced to ... [bring] in new recruits from the other side. It is impossible to detect these people ... when they arrive by train or boat and it is only by making a systematic regular inspection of these resorts, that detection can be made.[5]

Stella knew full well that she would be a prime target and began to give careful consideration to packing up and leaving. In October 19, 1910, Dr. Milne, the Dominion Medical Inspector and Immigration Agent in Victoria, arranged to deport "a few girls who were American citizens."[6] This was serious. Like some of her colleagues Stella could have married to avoid deportation—Peter was still around—but she decided to return to California, at least for a while.

But first there would be a party. It was October 23, Stella's 38th birthday, and the girls and Quong were preparing a lavish celebration at Herald Street in her honour. It was a pleasant, cool Sunday afternoon with a moderate southerly wind rustling the leaves, glorious in their autumn colours. Stella and Peter decided it was a nice day to be in the countryside so they drove out to Rockwood. Roy had been staying out at the house but he had come into town for the party. At 7:00 PM Stella phoned Herald Street to tell her friends that she and Peter would not be coming back right away and they should go ahead with the festivities. A short time later there came a second call, this one frantic and made by Peter, to say that there had been an accident and could someone get a doctor out to The Gorge immediately.

Dr. George Hall and Dr. Edward Hart both hurried out to be greeted by a dreadful scene. One room of the Rockwood residence was in complete disarray and on a blood-drenched carpet lay Stella, her feet and ankles a mess of bright blood, tissue, bone and black shot from an exploded shotgun cartridge. She was barely conscious and in shock. An ambulance was summoned and she was rushed to St. Joseph's Hospital. Peter accompanied her but was promptly arrested, protesting loudly that it was all a mistake and purely an accident.[7]

At the hospital, Stella, still bleeding profusely, was taken into the operating room where a skilled surgeon, Dr. Frank Hall (uncle of Dr. George Hall and the former owner of Stella's Herald Street house), assessed her situation. Fortunately, his colleagues had noted a near-empty bottle of whisky, another of gin and a vial of chloroform in the room, showing that Stella and Peter had been drinking and probably using the chloroform to obtain a hallucinogenic high.[8] This was critical information, for the amount of ether for the operation had to be increased to overcome the stimulation of the alcohol. When that was taken care of, Hall examined her injuries and regretfully decided he must amputate at least one of her legs. He knew Stella and her business and how devastating it would be to a woman whose appearance and mobility were essential to her livelihood. He thought the other leg could be saved. Despite her intemperate habits, she was a strong and reasonably healthy woman and there wasn't anyone in town who wasn't familiar with her iron will. She would survive.

Later that evening, Stella awoke in the recovery room, overcome with pain in her head and an awful sensation of nausea, and she immediately began to vomit. Somehow through the haze she learned of her loss but barely had time to take it in when the police insisted on interviewing her. She gave a brief statement to the effect that it was an accident and that Peter was not in any way at fault. She was taken back to the

St. Joseph's Hospital in Victoria, where Stella, who had been shot by her lover, had her leg amputated. [PRIVATE COLLECTION]

recovery room, the lights were dimmed and she battled alter-
nating bouts of vomiting and mind-numbing pain until she
fell into a fitful sleep.

By this time Roy had learned the news, sent telegrams to
Minnie and Harry and then headed out to Rockwood to survey
the shocking scene. Peter begged to go with him and to
explain how it happened but Roy, despite Stella's statement,
did not believe in his innocence and could not tolerate him
any longer. Minnie did not believe for one second that it was
an accident and immediately made plans to go to Victoria.
Harry, who was, among other things, a featherweight boxer,
was more than ready to give Peter a thrashing. In view of
Peter's past record of abusing Stella, the police laid charges
against him and he was remanded on $2,000 bail.

Stella's statement said that she and Peter were in the room
that her brother Roy occupied when he was staying in the
house. Peter had just lit a fire in the grate and noticed a shotgun that Roy kept for hunting. He decided to unload it by
pumping out the cartridges; one exploded and struck Stella,
who was sitting nearby, in the feet and legs. Peter made a
statement giving the same story and once again emphasized
that it was purely accidental. The police were not so sure.

Peter's known penchant for violence and Stella's condition led the police to bring him before Magistrate George Jay
on the following Tuesday. Provincial Police Superintendent
Frederick S. Hussey told the press that the authorities felt
another statement should be secured from Stella, as the first
was taken immediately after her operation and she might still
have been suffering from shock. They were giving her every

Stella's lover, Peter Jensen, who "accidentally" shot her in 1910. The police weren't so sure this was the truth.

opportunity but Stella stood by her initial account and backed it up with a declaration from Dr. Frank Hall that she was in quite a normal condition when she made her first statement. She even hired Tod Aikman to appear for Peter, and he was released. Not long afterward, he left town. Stella was alone again and minus part of one leg, her only souvenir of this ill-fated affair.

The accident put an end to any thoughts of moving back to California and Stella entered a long period of convalescence. Minnie came to help, as quickly she could, by train and boat. They set up a room in Rockwood, placing Stella's bed where she could look out over the garden. She was very weak from loss of blood, shock and the persistent nausea. A wooden frame was placed in the bed and she had to push the cotton-wrapped stump of her leg against it, to maintain the muscle tone. After that, she did exercises for the knee and hip joints, then the stump was massaged and bathed in a warm solution of sodium carbonate. Minnie kept Stella's strength up with cups of hot beef tea and in time she began to recover. Her only pleasure was the daily ration of spirits and champagne Dr. Hall had ordered, for its quieting effect on the stomach and to restore her appetite.

Once Stella had regained some strength, she had to learn how to walk with an awkward wooden leg and crutches. And she had to get back to business. It was very costly to maintain both houses and pay for her medical care. She was forced to mortgage both Herald Street and Rockwood to the B.C. Land and Investment Company for $3,000 to ease her financial burden. Minnie returned to Albuquerque—not a moment too soon as they were starting to get on each other's nerves.

Stella was not easy to get along with, in her pain and grief for the loss of her leg and, although she couldn't admit this to Minnie, for the absence of Peter.

Although struggling with her new disability, she was determined to get some money coming in; she put out the word that she needed girls and was soon back in business. Stella never had any trouble attracting girls to work for her because she was considered fair. This time the authorities backed off and no threats of deportation were levelled at her. Even the city officials showed a modicum of compassion and perhaps respect for this woman's strength and courage.

The year 1910 had been disastrous but, as calm always follows a storm, so it was for Stella. She learned to cope with the physical and emotional changes that had taken over her life and continued on in business: she had to live and it was all she knew. It was not until March 1911 that she was back in court.

With Tod Aikman helping her to rise, she stood painfully to answer charges of selling liquor, specifically wine, without a licence. This time she pled guilty and paid the $200 fine.[9] Though it was expensive at least she no longer faced the attempts at convicting her on the lesser charge of running a house of ill-fame. The fines for that were lower, but the raids and subsequent court appearances were a serious disruption; no one wanted the embarrassment of being exposed in court as a frequenter of a brothel. She gladly paid up and left the court, knowing she would probably not be bothered again for some time. In June she sold her Chatham Street house to Albert Goward, a manager of the BC Electric Railway Company, for $15,000.

In July Stella made her next court appearance, this time in the Saanich municipal police court, but still under the exasperated eyes of Magistrate George Jay. Once again she was accused of selling liquor without a licence. The police had gathered information by bringing in two detectives from Vancouver, D. F. Hewling and A. E. Verby, to pose as customers. The detectives testified that they had visited Stella's house on two separate occasions and each time they had bought liquor. Then came a great shock.

Across the courtroom, appearing for the prosecution, was Stella's trusted lawyer, Tod Aikman, who had recently been hired as the solicitor for the municipality. As Stella sat in stunned silence Aikman, in his usual eloquent manner, stated that Saanich was determined to have the house occupied by the defendant closed. He spoke of complaints from people residing in the area and declared that the morning's prosecution was merely the first step toward driving the occupants and habitués of the house from the district.[10]

He was true to his word. On the morning of Saturday, August 11, Stella and "a bevy of smartly dressed but heavily veiled young ladies" appeared in the court to hear charges, after a raid the night before. Nine arrests had been made, all women, which meant that the "frequenters," in this case baseball players, were not required to appear. The trial was adjourned for one week, during which Stella fumed and fretted over Tod Aikman's betrayal. What a fool she had been. It was clear that Aikman thought her days as a successful madam were over and there was little money to be gained from her. Why had she not learned that the last people she should place her trust in were men? They constantly let her down, except for Roy and Harry—but then, she and Minnie had raised them to be honourable men, and they were—most of the time.

The following Tuesday Stella appeared in court, barely containing her anger as a charge of keeping a disorderly house was read to her. Before she could even respond Constable Little crossed the floor and presented her with an amended charge that Aikman also handed to Jay. Stella took it from Little's hand, glanced at it, only to see that four additional charges of selling liquor without a licence had been added, and flung it violently onto the floor. Her new solicitor, Hume Robinson, fervently hoping to maintain calm, asked to see it. When the constable handed it to him, Stella grabbed it, tore it in half and handed it back. Aware that her fury was reaching the exploding point, Robinson tried to calm her but only made things worse. Immediately she was on her feet, banging her handbag on the rail and yelling for all to hear what she thought of the authorities. "Robbers, thieves, grafters," she shrieked and, in defiance of Jay, crossed the courtroom to the door, which she slammed several times as hard as she could. She was forcibly pulled away by the constable, who was likely rather thrilled at touching such a notorious woman.

Magistrate Jay who, over the years, had seen a lot of Stella and was surprised at nothing, calmly imposed a contempt-of-court charge and ordered that she be placed in the city jail for 24 hours. Robinson resigned. The eight young ladies paid their $50 fines and scattered. And Stella sat alone in the cell, nursing her fury, rubbing her painful leg and contemplating her predicament. Every time she thought of Aikman's weasel-like face and Magistrate Jay's smug demeanour she wanted to spit.

In court the next morning a calmer if not contrite Stella gritted her teeth as her solicitor, who had consented to return, apologized for her behaviour. The prosecution presented its case and then the defence (following Aikman's old tactics) argued that it had not been proven that Miss Carroll was the owner and occupier of the house. But Magistrate Jay did not accept this, stating that the evidence of Constable Little as to her occupation of the house and of other witnesses as to the character of the house was good enough for him.

Stella was convicted of being the keeper of a bawdy house and sentenced to four months' imprisonment with hard labour. For selling liquor without a licence she received the maximum fine of $250 on one count; the other charges were dropped as they occurred on the same day. The fine wasn't a surprise: the day before, August 23, Stella had mortgaged her Herald Street house to William Grant, the proprietor of the Windsor Hotel and Saloon, for $4,000 to cover the expected fine and her legal fees. What was unexpected was the jail sentence. However, it wasn't an immediate problem; no one was rushing her off to prison yet. An appeal was made to the provincial government, particularly as it was well known that Attorney General William Bowser was dead set against jail terms for this type of crime.

Her legal battles were proving costly and in September Stella called on Minnie for financial help. In exchange she conveyed to her a half-interest in Rockwood. Delays in getting the matter resolved only added to Stella's bad mood, and the rainy, cold weather hampered her ability to get around. She was to be taken into prison on November 24, but managed to get a delay.

However, at 6:40 PM on the cold, drizzly evening of December 4, Stella finally signed in at the jail. Her property as itemized consisted of only $5.50. It was a very low moment in her life but, with the constant reassurance of her solicitor, she held onto hope. Three hours later, armed with an order signed by Provincial Judge Peter Lampman, Robinson reappeared, smiling and waving the document to secure her release. Tired and very relieved, Stella signed out at 9:35 PM. Her usual signature, "E. Carroll," was large and scrawled in red ink.[11]

seven

When You are Married and Living at Your Ease,
Remember I am Single and Doing as I Please

IT HAD BEEN A CLOSE CALL and Stella was weary of the fight. She decided again to return to business but try to keep a low profile. Aikman may have won the court battle, but she was not finished. By now she was operating at both Rockwood and Herald Street, although she lived mainly at Herald Street—she didn't want to risk going up against Aikman again. It did mean travelling back and forth a lot but Stella, with her usual style, cut quite a dashing figure in her horse-drawn, four-wheeled phaeton with the top folded back and one of her many decorative bonnets covering her hair. It put her in mind of the mad dash for land in the Oklahoma Territory when she and Minnie, with little Harry between them, rushed to claim near their father and Roy. She found it amusing when one young police constable stopped her for driving her buggy on Craigflower Road without lights. She was fined five dollars.[1]

She continued undisturbed until early in the spring of 1912 when the members of the Purity League took it upon themselves to do something about this flagrant immorality. They kept watch on the Herald Street house and generally made it uncomfortable for those visitors who wished to remain anonymous. One reformer later testified that he had seen 28 men approach the house over a three-hour period and while 5 were turned away, the rest were let in. Mindful of this, the police formed a morality squad and brought in Frank

Stella in her buggy in front of Rockwood. She was a familiar figure to the police, who watched her race back and forth between her businesses. [PRIVATE COLLECTION]

Some of the "boys" from the Dixi Ross Company were said to frequent Stella's place. [BC ARCHIVES F-06965]

Williams and J. T. Cain, from the Vancouver branch of the Thiel Detective Agency, to conduct undercover work. Williams and Cain visited the house on four separate occasions, April 9 and 11–13. One night, the unsuspecting Stella even told them she had received an anonymous tip over the telephone that the house was going to be raided, and sent them away. Not surprisingly the raid was cancelled and set for the next evening.

At 11:00 PM on April 13, Deputy Police Chief Palmer, three sergeants and several constables knocked at Stella's door, which she cautiously opened just a crack; they broke the chain, poured in, served the warrant and began to sweep through the house.

Stella immediately phoned to Rockwood to say, "The house has been pinched" and rang off. A large quantity of liquor was found in an upstairs bathroom and 15 men were taken away with Stella, Quong, and two women, Nellie Foster, who was also known as Roma Grahame, and Bessie Moore. They were led down the front stairs and past a small group of moral reformers and neighbours who had been watching the house.

The next day Stella was charged with selling liquor without a licence and operating a disorderly house. Her bail was set at $2,000; Bessie and Nellie's was $500 each. Even poor Quong was assessed bail at $100. Stella paid her bail and left the others to languish in jail until their court appearance the following

Police mug shot of Nellie Foster a.k.a. Roma Grahame. She worked for Stella and later had her own brothel in Vancouver, B.C. Stella did not trust her. [VICTORIA POLICE MUSEUM AND ARCHIVES]

week, an act that did not endear her to them.[2] It was out of character for her to do this, as she was usually kind to her girls, and especially to Quong, but she was short of cash and she had never liked Nellie or Bessie anyway. Nellie in particular she considered a duplicitous and ambitious woman—not a person to be trusted.

On April 22 testimony commenced and Magistrate Jay sat back ready to listen, as if he hadn't heard it all before. Three constables, a sergeant and an inspector all testified as to their knowledge of the character of the house and Auguste Borde, the city's water-rate collector, stated that Stella was the person who paid the water charges and had for some years. Deputy Chief Palmer offered in evidence the warrant that had been used and each of the undercover detectives submitted notes on their visits to the house. Their testimony revealed that on several occasions, they had been welcomed to Stella's establishment and offered a price list of drinks and the sexual services of Nellie or Bessie. They had managed to refuse these without inviting suspicion and Stella even suggested they go to Rockwood where she had "plenty of girls" to choose from. She gave them a card with the directions and her signature that would gain them entry. They shared quite a few drinks with her and learned that business was good and that she was even thinking of running some gambling games or lotteries out of her place. Several men were observed arriving to drink, some to choose a girl, and the "accused" was constantly leaving to answer the door. Baskets with bottles of beer and whisky, trays with towels and liquor glasses were all offered in evidence. Stella's previous convictions were detailed, for both Herald Street and Rockwood.[3]

Quong's charges were dismissed and Nellie and Bessie were fined $50 each. Stella, in the face of overwhelming evidence of liquor consumption, pled guilty to selling liquor without a licence and was fined $250. She promptly wrote a cheque. When it came to the charge of keeping a disorderly house, Magistrate Jay had a speech prepared. He felt Stella had been treated leniently in the past with only a gradually increasing fine as a deterrent. She had not heeded the warnings and her persistent violation of the law could be stopped only by the imposition of a term of imprisonment. He gave her the maximum allowable, six months. As she was led from the court Stella stopped, turned to Jay, looked him in the eye and said sarcastically, "Goodbye, Your Honour."[4]

Of course, she appealed. Confident of the result, she was shocked when Provincial Judge Peter Lampman upheld the conviction. Nellie and Bessie, in exchange for the reasonable fine, had willingly given evidence as to the character of the house and testified they paid Stella five dollars a night for a room to be used for prostitution and any meals they wanted. Too late, Stella could see that not paying their bail had been a big mistake.

There was rejoicing in some circles. The *Times* gleefully reported the news:

CARROLL CASE FAILS; WOMAN IS IN PRISON
Judge Lampman Confirms Magistrate Jay's Conviction
Of Notorious Woman—After being many times before
the court on charges of keeping a bawdy house and
selling liquor on unlicenced premises ... Estelle

Durlin, alias Carroll, went to jail yesterday afternoon for six months imprisonment.[5]

A political broadsheet in Victoria was sardonic:

Stella should be glad of a six months rest during the warm weather, and show her gratitude by keeping mum on the boys who used to visit her. Give your mind to better things and live up to the promises you made, Stella, when you left the hospital. We will take care of the information given us when you thought of passing to the Great Beyond. It will be a sealed book on the boys, even if they were Cabinet Ministers, so long as they keep their promises to be good in the future.[6]

It wasn't a good week. She had to endure the embarrassing ride, accompanied by a young constable, from the jail to the harbour where she was placed on the first boat for the mainland; then she was taken to the prison at New Westminster. It was a long, exhausting trip for a woman with her disability and it was a complete farce. As she expected, when she arrived at the jail the warden was waiting with instructions directly from Attorney General Bowser, calling for her to be released immediately. She walked in one door and right out again, stopping only to freshen up and secure a cab to take her to the nearest hotel. The next day she was back on the boat for Victoria. Then, she had barely returned when she learned of the death of her old partner, Joseph Brown. It didn't look as though she would be going to the funeral because the press was lauding him as a highly respected resident of the city and it would not do to have a "notorious" woman among the mourners.[7]

It was time to put her business in order. The previous year Stella had given Roy power of attorney over her affairs, and as Minnie was now part-owner of Rockwood, she decided that she would do the same, so he could act on behalf of both of them. Stella and Minnie secured a mortgage from Henry Emmanuel Levy on the Rockwood property in the amount of $5,000 at the exorbitant rate of 18 percent, to cover Stella's ongoing financial problems.[8]

The fact that she was already back in town did not escape the eyes of the editor of the *Times*. Investigating further, he discovered that any women who were convicted of crimes of immorality and sent from the Victoria jail to the penitentiary in New Westminster were released on orders from the attorney general's department. Magistrate Jay's attempt at cracking down and instituting jail sentences rather than fines was apparently not working; the women ended up with no punishment at all, save for a rather inconvenient trip to New Westminster.

NOT ADMITTED TO PROVINCIAL JAILS—ADMINISTRATION OF JUSTICE AFFECTED

The attitude of the Attorney-General on the subject of the imprisonment of immoral women has caused the utmost consternation on the part of those acquainted with the circumstances ... By the action of the Attorney-General the Magistrate's hands are tied and his influence for good in Victoria is negatived ... As the hands of the magistrate are tied so are the hands of the police.[9]

Stella, who could have been toiling in the laundry at the jail, was instead busily making plans for her wedding. She had a new man in her life, another young one, 12 years her junior. George Edward Bearns was born in Newfoundland but his family had moved to British Columbia after the death of his mother. He had blue eyes, brown hair and the air of a charmer, much like Stella's earlier loves. Unknown to his intended bride, he had actually abandoned a wife in England, and was on poor terms with most of his family. George had various occupations but usually called himself a commission agent or accountant. He was known to get into the occasional bit of trouble, once being accused of stealing another man's pocket watch, but for the most part he behaved himself.

He and Stella were married on December 16, 1912, at St. Paul's Manse in Victoria with Roy Carroll and a friend, Ab Holmes, as witnesses. Stella was 40, George was 28.[10] As well as having a handsome young man for a companion, she now had protection from deportation. George had, he thought, a secure future with a wealthy woman who would spoil him, perhaps even mother him, with her generosity. And as a bonus she had a very open attitude toward sex.

Stella and George set up housekeeping at Rockwood. There were no more raids, no more court appearances and no fines for the next two years. These should have been calm and happy years, but Stella had once again chosen the wrong man.

One night, when George had had too much to drink, he began to berate Stella for nothing in particular; it was really out of his frustration that she was in control of "their" money. She tried to ignore him but the verbal taunts became

Stella with
George Bearns
(husband
number three)
at the Panama–
Pacific
Exposition in
San Francisco,
1915. Their
relationship
was already in
decline.
[PRIVATE
COLLECTION]

physical. When she pushed him away he threw her to floor and began to kick her. It was not easy to get back up with only one good leg but she managed, gave him another good shove and got to the phone to call the police, who quickly arrived to take him away. She still had her friends on the force. Sober and contrite, George was back the next day and Stella knew she would gain nothing by charging him in court. He was her legal husband and the courts didn't interfere in such relationships; besides she was an "immoral" woman and most people would think she deserved a beating.

Stella still had income from her rental properties, but she was seriously thinking again about leaving Victoria. She periodically ran the brothel but ironically, she had started renting rooms at Herald Street to men as boarding-house accommodation, just as Morley and Langley had suggested years before. George also brought in some money and to keep him from being too restless, they did some travelling in 1913.

On one of their trips they went to San Francisco to see Stella's old friend, Tessie Wall, who was having problems of her own. This visit was as much for Stella's business as for pleasure, though she was keeping her plans to herself. Being with George was less than a delight and she meant to get away to have a private chat with Tessie when she could leave him somewhere to amuse himself.

San Francisco was hosting the Panama-Pacific Exposition to commemorate the opening of the Panama Canal, and the city was alive with visitors from all over the world. Stella loved to attend fairs, parades and other such amusements. She dragged a less-than-enthusiastic George through the splendid exhibits and then to have their photograph taken, seated in a wicker carriage in front of a painted backdrop. George dutifully indulged her, knowing he was on tenuous ground.

He could never understand how someone with her disability could be so wilful and determined. God knows there were times when he just had to give her a backhand to remind her who was the man in the family. He had to be cautious, though; she wouldn't hesitate to berate him in public and she still held the purse strings.

When Tessie got together with Stella, she presented her former colleague with a financial proposition that she couldn't refuse. The love of Tessie's life and now husband, Frank Daroux, who was a political figure in San Francisco, had received an invitation from no less a person than the automobile magnate Henry Ford to sail to Europe aboard his Peace Ship. Ford's plan was to meet with world leaders in Europe and persuade them to stop the impending world war. One contemporary observer described it as "a sublimely screwy paragraph in American History."[11] All that aside, this chance to mix with the elite was an honour Tessie refused to miss. Daroux was not keen but promised that if his wife sold her brothel, which was a constant embarrassment to him, he would accept Ford's invitation. There was no doubt in Tessie's mind as to the best candidate to take over. She loved her fine building with its elaborate and expensive furnishings and if anyone would care for them as she had, it was Stella.

From Stella's perspective the timing was perfect. Thanks to Tod Aikman's betrayal she dared not open again in Saanich, and with her recent conviction and sentence of jail time

Victoria itself was too risky. Not much was happening in Victoria anyway, other than a good deal of talk about prohibition. If that law went through she was finished: the most beautiful women in the world wouldn't be enough to attract a clientele if there wasn't an ever-flowing supply of beer, whisky and champagne to go with them. Also, she was anxious to get away from George. He was nothing but a financial drain and she was weary of his violent attacks. She'd had enough of that with Dudley Curtis and Peter Jensen. In San Francisco, she felt a renewed sense of optimism and enthusiasm; she loved a challenge, and the chance to operate an upscale parlour house in such a sophisticated city was a dream come true. The women struck a deal.

Upon her return to Victoria, Stella packed up, leaving Rockwood for Roy and George to live in, and rented out the Herald Street house. Its value had declined severely and she eventually abandoned it; it was sold to one of her creditors for back taxes.

Stella was cautiously optimistic about her future. Tessie's brothel was certainly well located; 337 O'Farrell Street was in the heart of the uptown Tenderloin district and just three blocks from Union Square. However, no sooner had she arrived than she was greeted by a highly distraught and barely coherent, Tessie, drunk, who broke the sad news that Frank had betrayed her. He was not going to keep his promise and the whole Peace Ship exercise was becoming an embarrassing joke to Ford and everyone associated with it. As if that wasn't bad enough, Daroux was now threatening to divorce her. Stella lent a sympathetic ear but she had no intention of

Although their relationship was strained at times, Ben came to visit Stella when she moved back to San Francisco. Stella, of course, insisted on a photo. [PRIVATE COLLECTION]

returning to Victoria. She had come to San Francisco to run Tessie's brothel and she would not be dissuaded. Even Tessie didn't dare go against Stella's resolve but, unfortunately, she became an alcoholic fixture in the house. Although business went well for about a year, in the latter part of 1915 it got much worse.

Despite the World Exposition and the military camp at the Presidio, it was a bad time to move back to San Francisco. The moral-reform movement was growing and, with women's groups now having political influence, an intensive campaign against prostitution was on the horizon. Although Stella applauded the movement that had granted suffrage to women in California in 1911, it was undoubtedly having conse-quences for her business. In 1913 the state passed the Red Light Abatement Act, in part because of a campaign by the San Francisco YWCA and the local chapter of the Center of the California Civic League; the act targeted the owners of premises where prostitution was known to take place. Its back-ers hoped to rescue women from the sex trade by seeing the act enforced and providing alternative employment but they were disappointed. Of 40 women who were interviewed by one investigator

> ... 3 said they were willing to get married; 23 announced they would stay in their old line of business; 8 were going to join relatives; 3 were willing to work at honest employment; and 3 were undecided.[12]

By 1917 the cry to "clean out vice in San Francisco" had many powerful and articulate advocates. Methodist minister

Paul Smith, who was distressed to find that women were solic-
iting near his church at Leavenworth and O'Farrell streets,
joined other clergy and reputable apartment owners in the
area to protest. They were determined to at least keep the
women on lower O'Farrell Street, below Taylor. Luckily, this
was just where Stella was located. However, she was sadly mis-
taken if she thought she would finally be left in peace. Smith
and his cohorts insisted on touring the Tenderloin and
declared that over 25,000 persons there were profiting from
the proceeds of "vice." His attempts to push the authorities to
close the rest of the area were met with a backlash from the
women who worked there. They challenged him to a meeting
and he obliged, organizing one at the Dreamland Rink. He
expected a couple of hundred to attend but the papers reported
"thousands turned out and thousands were turned away."[13]

Before he knew it, the women, who had a more experienced world view, shouted down Smith's gentle suggestions of
faith and "Trust in God." One woman adamantly declared
they were safer and better off in this profession than in many
others; at least they had enough money to support their children, a difficult task on the minimum wage of eight dollars a
week for unskilled jobs. In the end Smith declared his sympathy:
"It has taught me many things, and for one, I shall work for a
minimum wage for women."[14]

Stella stood a discreet distance away, watching the goings-on
and thinking that it really was the end of her profession. She had
been around long enough to know that this was no temporary
setback; things were changing, and rapidly. For moral reform to
gain such strength in San Francisco, the party town, was truly

a portent of dire consequences for the Tenderloin. She had to operate a while longer for financial reasons, but with careful timing she hoped to get out before it was too late. Unfortunately, Tessie was her undoing.

Her marriage to Frank was on a downward spiral; he soon moved out and began an affair with another woman. Tessie continued to spend her time with Stella, consuming as much alcohol as she could and maintaining that she wasn't drunk until she couldn't walk. In March 1917 Stella phoned Frank after a particularly nasty scene with Tessie, and he and Tessie's brother Joseph had to take her away by force. Tessie's drinking, and obsessing about her husband's betrayal, eventually led to some very public confrontations which culminated in her buying a gun and shooting Frank three times in the chest; surprisingly, he survived. Divorce proceedings began in early spring and much to Stella's frustration there was a lot of testimony about 337 O'Farrell Street being a brothel, due to the condition Frank had placed on Tessie in 1915.

Between the Reverend Smith's campaign and Tessie's divorce, Stella had no chance to operate discreetly. She even called the brothel the "Hotel Thornton" to give it the air of a respectable lodging place but to no avail. (The site is now occupied by the highly respectable Hilton Hotel.) Using the Red Light Abatement Act, the police carried out systematic raids throughout the Tenderloin. In May, a massive sweep that included the Hotel Thornton netted 125 men, women and boys, all charged with violating morality laws. Police Judge Sullivan berated the detectives for the extensive raids saying, "What do you want me to do? Do you want me to poison them or shoot them?"[15] However, by the summer, judges were warning that anyone convicted of keeping a house of ill-fame would get a jail sentence and there would be no exceptions.

Business was brisk at Stella's because the Presidio teemed with lonely men, but she knew it was time to close down. She was suddenly tired of this life. She lived with chronic pain from the ulcerated stump of her leg, and now from her gall bladder. Her physician had warned her that women at her age—that is, in menopause—were prone to a general decline in health, particularly if they had led a life of indiscretion and excess in sexual passion, contraception, stimulating foods and, of course, alcohol. Stella snorted, "For once, I am guilty on all counts!"[16] Because her gall bladder was acting up, however, she couldn't think of moving on quite yet.

She stayed open, knowing it was risky, but luck wasn't with her. In October her place was raided and she was indicted under a federal act for selling liquor to soldiers in uniform (apparently they hadn't taken them off yet) and for keeping a house of ill-fame within five miles of a military encampment. Federal Judge William C. Van Fleet found her guilty on both charges and was not inclined to leniency based on her lawyer's plea that she was ill.

> This woman's physical condition did not appear to interfere with the lively and vicious business she carried on and with her exceedingly villainous traffic. She is a disgrace to her sex and lost to any sense of decency. I have not heard of a case of this kind in which I felt inclined to inflict the extreme penalty, but I do feel so

Stella left the "profession" at the end of the Second World War and moved to Alameda, California. She is ill, still on crutches and has narrowly escaped serving prison time. [PRIVATE COLLECTION]

in this case. Selling liquor to soldiers, in a certain sense is treason, and the penalty is entirely too small.[17]

Stella was sentenced to one year and a fine of $1,000. The judge offered to lessen this by two months and $250 if she would plead guilty. She did. The federal government had an agreement with the San Francisco courts that women convicted in such cases were to be sent to jail. Lieutenant Goff and his men were being hailed "for protecting the soldiers and sailors in this city" and soon women were being prosecuted under the federal Espionage Act. The military were evidently in dire need of saving from the likes of a sick, one-legged, 46-year-old woman. At this point it was all Stella had to laugh about and she did; her sense of humour was one of the many strong traits that had helped her to survive.

eight

Our Lives are Albums Written Through

TELLA COULD NOT FACE THE idea that she might actually spend a year in jail and for-tunately, she didn't have to.[1] When judges began sentencing under the federal laws, they apparently weren't aware, or didn't care, that there were no federal prison facilities for women. Instead, any female inmate was sent to one of the county prisons, which were hopelessly overcrowded. Some were put up in other institutions, such as hospitals, but eventually they were quietly turned out.

As Stella's finances were in serious decline, she may well have walked away from any equity she had in 337 O'Farrell Street.[2] To go from being a prosperous landowner and devel-oper to a woman with nothing was a major adjustment. All of her properties were gone, except Rockwood in Victoria, but that was now in the names of Minnie and Roy, to cover the debts she owed them. In fact Roy, who was still living there, had astonished the family by marrying a young "flapper," Maude Lena Thomson, known as Molly, who gave birth to a son, Roy Jr., a year later.

Stella wasn't totally down and out, though, and in 1920 she rented a large, ornate home in Alameda, across the bay from San Francisco and adjacent to Oakland. It was a good move because plans to construct a bridge across this piece of water would make access to San Francisco easier. Hearkening back to Mayor Morley and Police Chief Langley's advice many years ago in Victoria, Stella decided to open a boarding house for the men who were working in the nearby shipyards.

This turned out to be a success, since she was still surrounded by men who were impressed by her fastidious attention to detail and exemplary cooking. She did like to be appreciated by the male sex, and now she could put away the painful corsets and fancy fitted dresses and relax in a more comfortable housedress. She had put on weight with age and the loss of her mobility, but she was able to purchase a better wooden leg and could finally get rid of her uncomfortable crutches.

Fate had one last exciting experience for Stella. Among her boarders was a young man who had emigrated from Austria and was working in the Alameda shipyard. Unlike the other men in her life, Martin Fabian was shy and quiet. Stella soon found herself in love again. This gentle man reciprocated her feelings and she knew he would never raise a hand to her. On November 9, 1920, they were married at Minnie's house in Los Angeles with Minnie's new husband, a professional

Stella in front of the legitimate boarding house she ran in Alameda, California. By this time, the crutches were gone and so were the corsets. [PRIVATE COLLECTION]

gambler named Johnny Meeks, as a witness.[3] On the certificate, Stella stated this was her second marriage (in fact it was her fourth); it was the first for Martin. She was 48 and he was 35.

After the ceremony Minnie prepared a lavish steak dinner accompanied by a lot of champagne. She was sure that, just as she had found her true love with Johnny, Stella had found hers with Martin. After a few drinks they sat down to Minnie's wonderful dinner, and the usually reticent Martin, emboldened by alcohol, couldn't express his appreciation to Minnie enough, declaring her steak to be the best he had ever eaten. He didn't notice that his adoring new wife, sitting across from him, was starting to sizzle as well, until she burst out with "Is that so? Well, you have had your last steak dinner from me!" He did not make the mistake of praising Minnie over Stella again, and from that day on he became a little quieter.

Like Roy, Harry, at the age of 40, surprised everyone by getting married, to a woman named Winnifred in 1922. He had had a life of adventure, wandering and womanizing, taking on everything from featherweight boxing, under the name "Kid Carmen," to property development in Oregon. He claimed boxers Gentleman Jim Corbett, Jack Dempsey and Diamond Jim Brady, and actress Lillian Russell, as friends. He sold oil stocks in San Diego and timberlands in Oregon and was an inventor of sorts, with patents for, among other things, a steam-driven car. Now he was settled, in San Jose and later Long Beach, California, and in time had four children: William, Jack, Mary Minnie and Estelle. The girls were named for Harry's sisters.[4]

Despite the sisterly rivalry, the family had become much

Minnie with the
love of her life,
gambler Johnny
Meeks.
[PRIVATE
COLLECTION]

closer. Minnie and Johnny were firmly ensconced in Los Angeles where their father, Ben, and his wife, Mattie, also lived. There was much visiting back and forth as they were all great lovers of travel—camping, hunting, fishing and prospecting trips. Visits to Minnie's house always found the children raiding the large, cut-glass punch bowl, a relic from her brothel, that she kept filled with Hershey's Kisses, a sign of her ironic and ribald sense of humour. When the relatives came to visit Stella she would drive them out in her dark green Chrysler coupe to visit the giant redwoods in northern California.

Martin and Stella had moved and now rented a very attractive Queen Anne house at 1207 Santa Clara Avenue in

Stella loved to have her nieces and nephews (here, she is with Harry's children and Roy Jr.) come to visit. [PRIVATE COLLECTION]

Stella cuddling her namesake Estelle (Harry's daughter) and her sister Mary. If there was ever regret for her old lifestyle, it was probably in these moments. [PRIVATE COLLECTION]

Alameda. Martin left the shipyard for a job as a riveter on the construction crew for the Bay Bridge and Stella indulged her love of cooking, making preserves with the fruit from their trees and playing with her adored nieces and nephews and the family dog. For the first time in her life she was living simply and feeling completely happy. There were nights out, too. Martin's niece, Anna Elizabeth Huber, was a soprano with the San Francisco Opera and Stella was proud to attend her performances, as a nice affection had grown between them. Everyone was finally content.

Roy and Molly were happy to live at Rockwood with Roy Jr., now a toddler, and Roy continued to make his living as a barber.

Martin Fabian, Stella's fourth husband, and her nieces Mary and Estelle (Harry's daughters). Martin's untimely tragic death broke Stella's heart.
[PRIVATE COLLECTION]

On August 5, 1923, about 8:45 PM, Molly had just put little Roy to bed when both she and Roy became aware of smoke filtering down from the top of the house. Roy tore upstairs to investigate, only to find that a spark from the chimney had set the roof on fire. They grabbed little Roy and a few precious belongings and ran out into the yard. Fire brigades from both Saanich and Victoria were on their way and in time were joined by recruits from the Esquimalt naval base. Roy and a couple of neighbours pulled some of the furniture outside, managing to rescue sofas, carpets, two stoves and some smaller items, but the intense heat eventually forced them back. By 10:00 the main staircases collapsed and soon after that, the walls. Along with "hundreds" of onlookers, all they could do

The Carroll "girls" at the beach. L-R: Beatrice (Stella's half-sister), Winnie (Harry's wife), Minnie (with Jack, Harry's son) and Molly (Roy's wife). Stella is kneeling behind. [PRIVATE COLLECTION]

was watch helplessly as the house was totally consumed. The *Times* commented the next day, perhaps with a veiled reference to the house's shady past, that it "made a beacon that lighted up the country for miles around."[5] The loss was estimated at $26,500, although it was insured for only $7,000. Roy subdivided the land, building a small house on one lot, and selling the rest of the lots individually.

That was just the beginning of the turmoil. Roy and Molly moved back to the U.S., but Molly's health had been in decline for some time and in 1928 she passed away from tuberculosis. Roy was left with an eight-year-old son.

The siblings were all stunned by the loss of their pretty, lively sister-in-law, but their immediate concern was to help the little boy weather this painful event. They all congregated at Stella and Martin's place, where Roy Jr. was distracted by playing with his young cousins and Stella's dog. She even prepared his favourite breakfast, pancakes with her homemade preserves. As was often the case in those days, Roy turned to his sisters for help. Little Roy stayed with Stella and Martin for a few months and then spent some time with Harry and Winnie, but eventually he lived permanently with Minnie and Johnny.

When Ben Carroll died in 1931, Stella and Martin went to Los Angeles to attend the funeral. Like any Carroll event that included the two sisters, this one turned into an evening of drinking, with a little too much alcohol taken by some members of the family. As usual, Stella and Minnie began to argue and it escalated: glasses were thrown and a lamp smashed, and quiet Roy finally rose to his feet to intervene. Pushing one of

Always an independent woman, Stella loved to drive—except for the trip to the hospital after Martin's accident. [PRIVATE COLLECTION]

them into a corner of the couch and the other into a chair on the opposite side of the room he commanded them to stop, much to the amusement of the rest of the family.

Back in Alameda, Stella's life carried on happily with Martin, but after 12 calm years, a simple phone call on May 20, 1932, brought her contented world to an end. The police informed her that Martin had been hurt at work, on the construction of the Bay Bridge. She dashed to her car and rushed to the hospital but she was too late: Martin had died. For Stella, who had weathered many storms, this was the greatest heartbreak of all. After a strange life-journey of highs and lows, poverty and wealth, joy and pain, in the end she had found love and peace with Martin and the rest of the family. Now it would all come undone.

Johnny Meeks, Minnie's husband, with Stella in Victoria. Johnny was a gambler who was well known in Las Vegas and once managed a gambling ship moored offshore from Los Angeles and frequented by celebrities.
[PRIVATE COLLECTION]

Aside from her heart-rending grief, she had to face the loss of income. Martin was insured but the company challenged Stella's claim and refused to pay out, declaring they believed Martin had committed suicide. The coroner's report and death certificate stated very clearly that "death was due to natural causes," namely myocarditis, an inflammation of the heart muscle leading to heart failure; this had caused him to fall from the bridge. Despite this evidence, Stella was never able to collect. She was forced to give up the house in Alameda and become a housekeeper for a pig farmer in Hayward, looking after his two little girls. Her life was lonely and difficult and Minnie, in an attempt to cheer her, suggested they take a trip to Victoria.

They were soon on the road—Minnie, Johnny, Stella and Trixie, her current dog. Filled with recollections and mixed emotions, Stella strolled around what was left of Rockwood's gardens. It was unbelievable that the beautiful house was gone and these small bungalows now occupied the grounds of the former estate. So many memories. Perhaps she could drop in on Magistrate Jay or even better, former Mayor Morley. How had it gone so wrong? Perhaps she shouldn't have left; really, it was Aikman's fault but he was gone too, taken by heart disease just like her beloved Martin. Victoria was quite a sedate town now, very pretty with its hanging flower baskets (initiated by, of all people, Morley), gracious gardens, the Parliament Buildings and the stately Empress Hotel. She remembered when it officially opened, with all the dignitaries and journalists in town, including that bounder, Brewer, who had cost her so much money with his bad cheque.

Irritating though Minnie could be, Stella was grateful for this trip. She knew she would never return and it was good to see the old places, although she felt a distinct shiver as she passed the hospital where she had lost her leg. Strange to think that Rockwood was gone while the Herald Street house was still standing and even the Duck Block, where poor Marval Conn had met her end. The buildings in Victoria hadn't changed much, but the city was slower and quieter.

Well, like Victoria, she was slower and infinitely quieter too. It was time to find a pleasant place to live out her remaining years. She gave some thought to staying in Victoria but that would be too far away from the family and, despite her nostalgia and appreciation of the gardens and parks, Stella knew there were too many painful memories there.

Stella with Trixie in the garden at Rockwood on a return visit to Victoria.
[PRIVATE COLLECTION]

In Lakeport, California, in 1943, 70-year-old Mrs. Fabian bent down slowly and painfully to refill the cracked bowl she used for her cats. She was tired and chilly; the house was quite drafty and it was only March. Leaning on her cane she hobbled first to a small table and picked up a white envelope, her fountain pen and a pencil, then went to her shabby chair, and sat down heavily. Using the arm of the chair as a desk she began to write, "My Autograph Album Given to me 1886 by My Mother. Estella F. 1943."

She picked up the small book, whose burgundy leather cover was faded and worn at the edges. The gold still stood out brightly and the portrait of the Victorian girl was scratched but clear. The pages were coming loose so she was careful to keep them in order as she opened the front cover. She searched her mind to recall the details of her mother's delicate features as she read her dedication, but they had faded. A sense of her quiet, gentle nature lived on, though, through her small, even handwriting, "November 23, 1886 To My Darling Stella—On your red lips, my love, lingered a smile. Though friends may flatter—Though life be gay, Do Not Forget Me When I'm Far Away. From TAC," and in small script below, "From Mama." In contrast there was a large pencil- scrawled notation: "I Have Not Aug. 1937 E.H.F. Gone Many Years Ago March 1887." She would never forget her. She had to do some calculation to remember she was only 14 the last time she had seen her mother. It seemed such a long time ago and many worlds away.

As she continued through the book the memories flooded back, helped by the pencilled notations she had made just six

Stella's house in rural Lake County, California, as it appeared in 1994. It was plain and humble, but it was in the country and she had her cats and rabbits for company.
[COURTESY OF KATHERINE LEWIS]

years ago. Her Aunt Minnie Bennett, now also gone, emphasized her mother's words, "Always remember the giver [of this book]. She was always loving and true to her dear ones." It all seemed confused now with other images and emotions. Tearful goodbyes with Uncle Billy and Grandma Araminta, Uncle Dennis and Aunt Laura, her cousins and all her friends flashed through her mind. Then there was the dreadful trip west to Kansas in the winter cold, while she and Minnie tried valiantly to keep rambunctious little Harry amused. The sod house—oh, God—the sod house, never again. Minnie's droll inscription, "Dear Sister—Make new friends but keep the old. The first is silver but the latter gold.

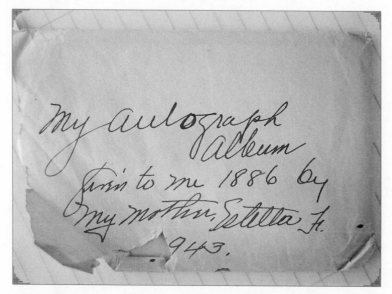

Stella kept her precious autograph book in this envelope. [PRIVATE COLLECTION]

It's a long long way to Tipperary & to dear old Kansas. Lovingly Sister M." Dear old Kansas indeed. And dear old friends—well, there was that storekeeper and Kirsey, he was sweet to me. Stella added another pencil notation. "Yes dear Sis I have had both & a heartfull. EHF." More memories—Roy sneaking in to write in her book about "cow boys" and little Harry "writering" on the bed. And who wrote "Foolish Misses Loose Their Kisses in a Free & Easey Way"? No signature but a date—Aug. 15, 1891. Must have been in Newkirk; someone who could see the future, no doubt. "Isn't it the Truth Ha Ha EHF," Stella wrote, smiling to herself.

There were no entries through the later 1890s, nothing until 1905. She had, of course, been very busy with two marriages: Curtis, God knows where he ended up, and Durlin, another mistake. The heady feeling of property deals going well and San Francisco, what a town! Ironic that that was where she got into the business and where she left, upon invitation from a federal court judge. Tessie and Frank: what a fool she had been for that man. And going further back, Lou Graham in Seattle; it had been wise to give up there, she had the town sewn up. And that damn Bessie Moore and Nellie Foster, as she was calling herself, almost had her in jail. Victoria, a charming town with the biggest bunch of two-faced politicians she had ever encountered. Well, she was a registered Democrat now; she had enough of that "conservative" hypocrisy in Canada.

And her beautiful house on The Gorge. Tragic to think it was all gone. Oh, and one inscription from that rascal George.

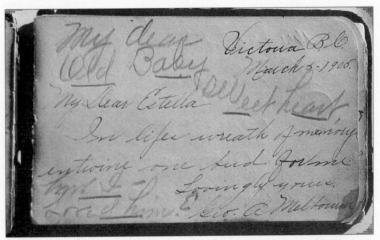

George Melbourne left a message in Stella's book. He broke her heart and left her in a foul mood. [PRIVATE COLLECTION]

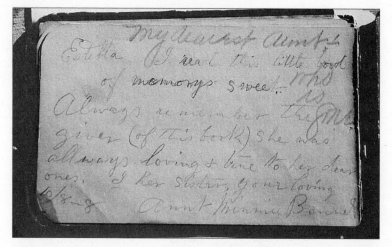

Tilly's sister, Minnie Bennett, worried about what would become of the children after their mother's death. She wrote this inscription to remind Stella of her mother's loving and "true" ways. [PRIVATE COLLECTION]

"Victoria, B.C. March 5, 1905 My Dear Estella In Your life's wreath of memory entwine one bud for me. Lovingly yours, Geo. A Melbourne." Oh yes, she would never forget George. Again her pencilled scrawl framed his words. "My Dear <u>old Baby Sweetheart. How I loved him.</u> E." Too bad he had to leave. Then she took up with Jensen, and now was missing part of a leg. If it hadn't been for Aikman and Jensen, she might still be at The Gorge with two good legs. But probably not.

Another from Minnie—no date but looks early, probably Kansas again. "A way back here out of sight I'll write my name just for spite." It brought Stella some grief to think of Minnie now. They had had one too many of those alcohol-driven fights and they hardly saw each other anymore. The years of frustration, the abuses they had both suffered, the secret envy, jealousy and blame and, of course, the money problems had taken their toll. Minnie and Johnny were a family with Roy Jr. while Stella lived by herself. Minnie buzzed around shopping, visiting, staying in touch with the family in Missouri and their half-siblings from Ben's marriage to Mattie. Minnie was the pretty one, the funny one, the one everybody loved. *I am alone*, thought Stella. *The damn leg is wearing me down and the pain in my gall bladder burns continuously.* She was about to sink into full-blown self-pity when she heard a scratch at the door. Another of the cats wanting to be let in. It was much nicer to be greeting them than those hypocrites Morley, Jay, Langley and that turncoat, Aikman! Hers was a quiet life, occasionally lonely, but it was nice to have the time to reflect on her full and eventful life. She had outlived them all except Morley—who was just too stubborn to die.

She knew she had been determined and tough, maybe even difficult, but she had fought her way out of poverty, achieved her goal of a superlative parlour house and had 12 happy, peaceful years with Martin. How many women could say that?

Stella struggled carefully to her feet, slid the little book back into the envelope and placed it in a drawer. She picked up her glass, got the bottle down from the shelf, shooing a cat onto the floor, and poured herself a drink, the only painkiller that really worked. Stella couldn't help but smile to herself as she thought, *Finding pretty girls used to be my profession; wouldn't people here be shocked. Oh well, no one knows me now and the cats don't care. There is no judgment here. Yes, this body was once strong and firm, with beautifully sculpted curves covered by the finest of handmade lace. Now, like that favourite old lace dress, both body and spirit are worn out, but what a journey they have had.*

Three years later, Lakeport had become a quiet retreat for tired souls seeking respite from day-to-day living in San Francisco and the growing metropolitan areas around it. The population swelled seasonally and changed the feeling from that of an out-of-the-way town to a recreation area. When the visitors left at the end of the summer the permanent residents continued on with their unhurried way of life.

For Katherine Lewis, a young graduate nurse and one of the permanent residents, it was a lovely, peaceful area that afforded her an opportunity to gain more experience in the operating room at the local hospital. During her usual trips to the Lakeside Hospital she passed the home of an elderly woman, Mrs. Fabian, who lived alone with only her cats as companions. When she heard that Mrs. Fabian had only one leg and was having problems with ulcers caused by the artificial leg, kind-hearted Katherine began stopping in to help her with cleaning and dressing the wounds. To Katherine, Mrs. Fabian was a pathetic figure: thin and frail, she seemed cut off from society. The house she rented was a small frame cottage, poorly furnished, with only plain wooden floors, and she had little comfort.[6] The younger woman had no way of knowing anything about her patient's rich and colourful past life.

On her last visit Katherine found Stella in terrible pain, not from her leg, but from her chronic gall bladder condition. She rushed her to the hospital but, despite attentive care, her condition steadily declined over a period of four weeks. Minnie and Johnny came to be by her side, but it was clear that the strength of body, mind and spirit that had carried Stella on so indomitably was finally exhausted. As her muscles relaxed and her mind cleared Stella's last physical sensation was the pressure of Minnie's hand on hers. She left a life that had been thoroughly experienced: she had seen and known the world in a way that few women of her time could have done.

On April 19, 1946, the *Lake County Bee* reported that "aged Matron" Estella Fabian had died. Although reported to be 71 she was in fact 73. She wouldn't have minded. After a modest funeral her body was conveyed to Santa Rosa for cremation and then to the Forest Lawn Cemetery in Los Angeles.[7] Her ashes now lie under a small marker that says simply: "Estella Carroll Fabian—Beloved Sister."

When all was said and done, Stella's grave marker showed her greatest achievement: "Beloved Sister." [COURTESY OF FOREST LAWN MEMORIAL PARK, GLENDALE, CALIFORNIA]

Epilogue

Stella's last years were characterized by poverty, loneliness and pain, and some of her contemporaries may have thought it a fitting retribution for a life of sin. Undoubtedly she was a woman who caused trouble and perhaps it can even be said she was a victimizer—not, as was often asserted by the newspapers of the day, of "respectable young men" but rather of the women she chose to employ and profit from. But it can also be said that she was a strong, intelligent, independent woman trying to make her way in the world, and had many times been a victim herself. She was a survivor. In terms of material wealth, she achieved much more than would have been expected for a woman from a small, rural Missouri town, and despite the difficult years at the end, she lived the life she wanted.

One constant in her life was her closeness with her family, born of shared experiences and a common outlook and philosophy; not everyone approved of it but it suited them. Even at the end, they remained close. Near Stella, in the cemetery, are the graves of Ben and of Minnie, who died in September 1955, six months after her husband, Johnny Meeks. Roy died in 1962 and his grave is close by as well.[1] Only Harry, who also died in 1962, is apart from his siblings, at the cemetery at Rancho Palos Verdes.

Possibly Stella's greatest achievement, although it is an intangible, is the measure of control she was able to maintain over her life. She had her own money, which allowed her to set up a business and live where she chose, and to divorce or move on from an abusive or opportunistic husband or lover when necessary. She kept her own moral code and fought to defend her rights as she saw them. Perhaps her old Kansas shopkeeper beau, Powells, captured it best when he wrote in Stella's book in 1887:

> *Dear Estella*
> *Our lives are albums written through*
> *With good or ill with false or true*
> *And as the blessed Angels turn*
> *The pages of our years*
> *God grant they read the good with smiles*
> *And blot the bad with tears*
> *Sincerely yours*
> *P M Powells*

Brothels, from the most elegant parlour house to the meanest and most sordid of cribs, exist and survive, as all businesses do, in response to consumer demand. For Stella, being a madam was a profession and what she understood best. Entrepreneurship was a quality not prized or encouraged in women at the turn of the last century, but Stella Carroll reached the top in the work she chose and had a hell of a time along the the way!

Glossary

BAWDY HOUSE — A brothel. In law, usually noted as "common bawdy-house." It comes from the French word *baud*, to be merry, which referred to a prostitute or sexually immoral woman.

BROTHEL — A house of prostitution. From an old English word originally referring to a ruined person and not an establishment: brothern.

BUNCO-MAN — A swindler or con man, also known as a "rounder."

CALLER — A male customer at a parlour house.

"COMPANY, LADIES" — These words, usually accompanied by the ring of a bell, would let prostitutes know that customers had arrived.

CARBOLIC ACID — A substance distilled from coal tar and used as a disinfectant. Prostitutes used it for contraception and to prevent disease. It was also taken orally to commit suicide.

CRIB — A small room or cabin where a prostitute worked.

DEMIMONDE — A class of women of "dubious" reputation who had joined the sisterhood of prostitution; also, a district where prostitutes worked.

DISORDERLY HOUSE — A house of prostitution or brothel.

FREQUENTER — In law, usually applied to the customers of the brothel although some employees, such as the cooks, house-keepers and musicians, were charged using this term.

HABITUÉ — A regular customer or frequenter of the brothel. Sometimes used to denote the prostitutes themselves.

HOUSE OF ILL-FAME — A house of prostitution, a brothel.

INMATE — A prostitute working in a brothel.

KEEPER — The manager/owner of a brothel.

LADIES OF EASY VIRTUE, OF JOY, OF THE EVENING, OF THE NIGHT — All terms for prostitutes.

LANDLADY OR LANDLORD — Outside of the standard definition, also denotes the manager of a brothel.

LINE — A term for the prostitution district in a small logging or mining town. The line itself usually consisted of one or many rows of small houses along a narrow street at the edge of town.

MADAM — The female manager and/or owner of the brothel. She fulfilled many roles as bookkeeper, chief hostess and "mother" to her girls. The best madams ran efficient houses and were privy to many secrets.

NECESSARY EVIL — One view of prostitution as a means of deterring rape and protecting "decent" women.

PARLOUR HOUSE — A high-class, even refined, house of prostitution.

RED-LIGHT DISTRICT — The area or district of a town or city housing prostitution. The term is said to come from Dodge City, Kansas, where railroaders hung a red lantern on the door of an occupied prostitute.

RESORT — A house of prostitution.

RESTRICTED DISTRICT — A district of prostitution. In many towns and cities in the Northwest, prostitution was tolerated if contained in a certain neighbourhood or area.

SOCIAL EVIL — Prostitution.

SOILED DOVE — A prostitute. Often just "dove."

SPORTING HOUSE — A house of prostitution, from the original meaning of an inn where sporting men would gather.

TENDERLOIN — The red-light district of a city or town. Originally referring to an area within New York City that was host to a great concentration of brothels, gambling dens, saloons and low theatres.

WHITE SLAVERY — The transport of young women or men for sexual purposes between countries.

Endnotes

CHAPTER ONE

1.   Autograph book—Estella Carroll, Carroll Family Collection. This autograph book was given to Stella when she was 14. She kept the book with her all her life, adding autographs and her own comments to it over the years. Each chapter title is an excerpt taken from this book.

2.   Abbott, F. W., "Limitation of the Family," *Massachusetts Medical Journal* (1890) quoted in Haller and Haller, *The Physician & Sexuality in Victorian America*, p.116.

3.   There are many labels for places where prostitution is conducted. The more common of these terms and the ones that appear most regularly in court and police records are "bawdy house," "house of ill-repute," "disorderly house" and "brothel." See Glossary.

4.   Elliott, Eugene Clinton, *History of Variety—Vaudeville in Seattle*, p. 52. Victoria was part of a vaudeville circuit that included Spokane, N. Yakima, Everett, Bellingham, Portland, Tacoma and Vancouver. Albini the Magician was Herbert Albini, a.k.a. Abraham Laski, a master magician and illusionist who specialized in card tricks.

5.   *Times*, August 16, 1911, p. 18.

6.   *Times*, August 11, 1911, p. 20.

7.   *Times*, August 14, 1911, p. 18.

CHAPTER TWO

1.   Obituary—William G. Carroll, 1905, private collection.

2.   U.S. Census Record—1880 Federal Census for Missouri, Crawford County, Boone Twp., ED 53 Fam. #159 p. 31A.

3.   Missouri, 1st Annual Agriculture Report, p. 59, pp. 162–3.

4.   Gerlach et al., *Atlas of Missouri*, p. 8.

5.   Missouri State Gazetteer and Business Directory, 1876–77. Crawford County, with a population of almost 11,000, had 1,265 farms, most of which were for raising stock because of the less than ideal conditions of the soil for crops. A secondary occupation in the area was mining.

6.   Toward the end of the 19th century some of these caves were developed for commercial tourism. Missouri has since become known as the "State of Caves," and childhood wonder at this curiosity was featured in Missourian author Mark Twain's novel *Tom Sawyer*.

7.   Correspondence, Emma Comfort Dunn to Linda Eversole, May 26, 1992.

8.   Autograph book—Estella Carroll, entry from Tilly Carroll dated November 23, 1886.

9. Telephone interview—Linda Eversole with Mary Rood, October 29, 1998.

10. *Garden City Irrigator*, September 30, 1886, quoted in *West of Wichita: Settling the High Plains of Kansas, 1865–90*, by Craig Miner, Lawrence, Kansas: University Press of Kansas, 1986, p. 182.

11. Autograph book—Estella Carroll, entry by P. M. Powells dated January 9, 1887.

12. *The Lane County Historical Society Presents the Lane County Bachelor*, Dighton, Kansas: Lane County Historical Society, n.d. Quoted in *West of Wichita*, p. 150.

13. Correspondence, Mary Rood to Linda Eversole, March 29, 1999.

14. *West of Wichita*, pp. 190–91.

15. Autograph Book—Estella Carroll, entry from Roy Carroll dated January 14, 1887.

16. Tefertiller, Casey, *Wyatt Earp: The Life Behind the Legend*, p. 268. "Cowboys would continue to be romanticized through the decades, the previous connotation lost to history."

17. Correspondence, Roy Carroll Jr., to Linda Eversole, January 22, 1999.

18. Autograph book—Estella Carroll, entry by Harry Carroll, n.d.

CHAPTER THREE

1. Brigham Young University, Special Collections, Western Historical Marriage Records—Curtis and Carroll, November 19, 1894.

2. *Winslow Mail*, June 20, 1896.

3. Autograph Book—Harry Carroll, private collection.

4. Correspondence, Mary Rood to Linda Eversole, March 29, 1999.

5. Arizona State Archives, Divorce record—Curtis vs. Curtis, July 14, 1896.

6. Arizona State Archives, Court record—Territory of Arizona vs. D.W. Curtis, Assault to Murder, 1896.

7. Marriage Certificate, Benjamin Carroll and Mattie Martin—Claremore, Indian Territory, May 9, 1896, private collection.

8. *Winslow Mail*, June 13, 1896. State of Ohio—Bureau of Vital Statistics, Certificate of Death—Dudley W. Curtis. Curtis eventually went back to Columbus, Ohio, where he died in 1914.

9. *Winslow Mail*, July 18, 1896.

10. *Winslow Mail*, July 3, 1897; Brigham Young University, Special Collections, Western Historical Marriage Records—Durlin and Carroll, June 27, 1897.

11. Gentry, Curt, *The Madams of San Francisco*, p. 222.

12. Asbury, Herbert, *The Barbary Coast*, p. 233.

13. Wolsey, Serge G., *Call House Madam*. This is purported to be the story of the career of Beverly Davis, a well-known Los Angeles madam who started her career working in the brothel of Tessie Wall's rival Jessie Hayman. Price comparisons have been made with various newspapers and the *Hudson's Bay Company Catalogue—*

Autumn/Winter 1910–11 (Reprint, 1977) and *The T. Eaton Co. Ltd. Catalogues—Spring & Summer, Fall & Winter*, 1901.

14. Ibid., Wolsey, pp. 55–56.

15. Identity records in both the Victoria and Vancouver police collections show that many of these women had convictions in several cities. In fact, police departments routinely exchanged copies of their identity records when they knew a convicted prostitute would be moving on to another city.

16. Correspondence, Mary Rood to Linda Eversole, March 29, 1999.

17. San Francisco may have been the premier city on the west coast, but it was also a marketplace in which the need for her business was already being adequately met. The courts would often make leaving town an alternative to a hefty fine or imprisonment. In order to escape the scrutiny of the authorities, and to find a new clientele, the working women followed a circuit, travelling on to other cities and smaller communities in both the United States and Canada.

18. Meier, Gary and Gloria, *Those Naughty Ladies of the Old Northwest*, pp. 58–63.

CHAPTER FOUR

1. Turner, Robert D., *The Pacific Princesses*, p. 54. The steamship *City of Seattle* was sold to the Pacific Coast Steamship Company and the *City of Kingston* sank in 1899.

2. BC Archives, BC Attorney General, GR 1327, B2377, 117/99 Inquisition—Marval Conn alias Ashton. BC Archives, BC Supreme Court (Victoria) GR1304, File 2208, Probate of Emma L. Johnson. Marval's real name was Emma Louisa Johnson. Upon her death it was revealed that she had been married and had one adult son. Both her son and her father came to identify her body and return her to the U.S.

3. BC Archives, GR 1900 Chattel Mortgages Vol. 3, pp. 727 and 737.

4. *Colonist*, August 3, 1877, p. 3. Simeon Duck's political career was the source of controversy on several occasions but he was a popular character in Victoria and any small indiscretions were usually overlooked.

5. In April 1886 Duck's name was on a list of owners of property rented out for prostitution, prepared by Police Chief Bloomfield. Madam Josie Williams and three girls were in residence at that time. Later on Duck rented to Vera Ashton. (Chief Bloomfield to D. W. Higgins, Chairman of the Police Committee, Victoria City Archives, VF-Prostitution.)

6. Canada, Census—1901—Victoria.

7. Autograph book—Estella Carroll, entry from George A. Melbourne, March 5, 1905.

8. Postcard, Minnie Carroll to Stella Carroll, March 16, 1903.

9. Obituary—William G. Carroll.

10. Postcard, Stella Carroll to Minnie Carroll, October 15, 1905.

11. *Columbian*, December 24, 1890, quoted in Turner, George H. *Before the Council; or Social Life in Victoria.*

12. *Colonist*, January 18, 1906, p. 4.

13. *Colonist*, January 19, 1906, p. 1.

14. *Times*, January 14, 1908, p. 6.

15. *Colonist*, January 25, 1906, p. 5.

16. *Colonist*, January 27, 1906, p. 5.

17. Postcard, Estella Carroll to Minnie Carroll, January 28, 1906. Private collection.

18. *Colonist*, September 25, 1906, p. 6.

19. BC Archives, GR1566, B7059 Victoria—Supreme Court Orders Folio 482 Dec. 6, 1906, Durlin vs. Slater and Phair.

20. *Colonist*, February 16, 1906, p. 7. Schoolteacher and trustee Agnes Deans Cameron was involved in a controversy surrounding the use of rulers in drawing. She lost her job over this issue.

21. Quoted in Gentry, Curt, *The Madams of San Francisco*, pp. 194–95.

22. Victoria Police Archives, Charge book—Volume 18, Folio 290, August 31, 1906.

23. *Colonist*, September 30, 1906, p. 8.

24. *Colonist*, December 11, 1906, p. 1.

25. Postcards, Stella Carroll to Minnie Carroll, October 16, 1906; October 20, 1906; November 24, 1906.

26. *Colonist*, December 11, 1906, p. 1.

27. *Colonist*, December 30, 1906, p. 2. Apparently these donations were a regular part of her routine. *Times,* January 7, 1908, p. 9.

28. *Colonist*, January 17, 1907, p. 4.

29. *The People's Press*, January 15, 1907, p. 1.

30. *Colonist*, January 17, 1907 p. 4.

31. Postcard, Estella Carroll to Minnie Carroll, March 3, 1907, private collection.

32. Biggerstaff Wilson was a prominent citizen from an old family, the son of William Wilson of W. and J. Wilson, Clothiers. He was annoyed at this infamous woman disrupting his plans and through some kind of finagling they reached an agreement whereby he advanced money to her to give up the property and establish her business farther up Herald. He in fact paid the taxes for her new brothel property in 1908. Victoria City Archives, City Assessment Roll, 1908.

33. Victoria Police Archives, Bulletin No. 50, May 13, 1907. "Instructions to all Members of Police Force."

34. *Colonist*, July 24, 1907, p. 2. This story made a nice bit of melodramatic copy, for which the *Colonist* was quite well known.

35. *Colonist*, July 25, 1907, p. 11.

36. Postcard, Stella Carroll to Minnie Carroll, July 6, 1907.

37. Victoria Police Archives, Bulletin, November. 29, 1907. "Instructions to Members of the Police Dept."

CHAPTER FIVE

1. *Times*, December 21, 1907, p. 4.

2. *Times*, December 24, 1907, p. 1.

3. *Times*, January 8, 1908, p. 9. Rumours abounded for years that a tunnel existed between the Union Club and either Seymour's or Morris's. No evidence of this has ever been discovered, and it seems unlikely; they were only a short walk away.

4. *Colonist*, February 29, 1908, p. 6.

5. Victoria Police Archives, Mug Shot Book #2, 1904–09, #513—F. C. Brewer.

6. *Colonist*, January 24, 1908, p. 6.

7. *Colonist*, February 29, 1908, p. 6.

8. At the time, Sylvestria was married to another individual of note, Oregon Columbus Hastings, an early astronomer and photographer who built an observatory in the top of his house. Perhaps Oregon was able to find an alternative use for his telescope, keeping an eye on Stella's place.

9. Victoria City Archives, Minutes of City Council, February 17, 1908, p. 708; Health and Morals Committee Report—February 21, 1908, CRS-4, City Clerk's Office, Committee Reports 1885–1956, Box 10. The committee, made up of William A. Gleason, Frederick Pauline, A. Henderson, John Meston and H. Norman, noted that the owner of said house had been cautioned several times that the house could not be used for immoral purposes. They recommended a special officer be stationed outside the house to take the names of all persons entering and leaving.

10. *Times*, March 4, 1908, p. 5.

11. Ibid.

12. Ibid.

13. Postcard, Stella Carroll to Minnie Carroll, April 5, 1908.

14. *Times*, June 27, 1908, p.1.

15. Ibid., p.7.

16. Ibid., p.1.

17. *Times*, June 29, 1908, p. 5.

18. BC Archives, GR0419, Vol. 129, Folio 1908/127 Estella Carroll—Notice of Appeal, British Columbia Attorney General, Documents. This successful writ of certiorari had an effect that is still felt today. Unless it is proved that the accused have direct knowledge that prostitution is taking place, they cannot be convicted. This situation makes conviction of owners of escort agencies and massage parlours difficult, if not impossible. *Times*, July 15, 1908, p. 2.

19. *Times*, July 22, 1908, p. 12.

20. Victoria Land Titles Office.

21. Wolsey, Serge, *Call House Madam*, p. 282.

22. *Colonist*, November 8, 1909.

23. *Times*, November 11, 1909.

24. Victoria Police Archives, Mug Shot Book #2, #668—Peter Jensen.

CHAPTER SIX

1. BC Archives, GR-784—British Columbia, Commission on Victoria Police Commissioners, 1910.

2. *Colonist*, April 10, 1910, p. 2.

3. Commission, 1910.

4. BC Archives, Central Immigration Files, White Slave Traffic Reports, 1909—41.

5. Ibid.

6. Victoria City Archives, Board of Police Commissioners, Minutes 1893—1909.

7. *Colonist*, October 25, 1910, p. 17.

8. Weil, Dr. Andrew and Rosen, Winnifred, *From Chocolate to Morphine*, p. 78 "Years ago, people sometimes sniffed the fumes of liquid chloroform or swallowed small amounts in order to experience what disapproving critics called 'a cheap drunk.'"

9. Victoria City Archives, Police Court Records—Magistrates Record Book, 1909—11.

10. *Times*, July 7, 1911, p. 5.

11. BC Archives, GR-662, Victoria Jail 1904—14, Prisoner's Charge and Sentence Book, December 4, 1911.

CHAPTER SEVEN

1. Victoria Police Archives, Charge Book, Vol.22, Folio 242, April 9, 1912.

2. Victoria Police Archives, Charge Book, Vol.22, Folio 252, April 14, 1912.

3. Victoria City Archives, Magistrate Record Books, 16D4, Folio 248; *Colonist*, April 14, 1912, p. 6, April 16, 1912, p. 13, April 23, 1912, p. 6; *Times*, April 15, 1912, p. 12, April 23, 1912, p. 11.

4. *Colonist*, April 24, 1912, p .6.

5. *Times*, June 14, 1912, p. 16.

6. Victoria City Archives.

7. *Times*, June 21, 1912, p. 7. Obituary, Joseph Brown. Former Police Commissioner Leonard Tait, who had figured prominently in the provincial commission investigation of 1910, was one of the pallbearers. *Colonist*, June 23, 1912, p. 7.

8. Victoria Land Registry Office, Charge Book Vol. 22, Folio 331, No. 5717G January 30, 1912, cancelled October 29, 1912.

9. *Times*, November 8, 1912, p.16.

10. Province of British Columbia, Ministry of Health, Division of Vital Statistics, Verification of Marriage Particulars, George Edward Bearns and Estelle Hannah Durlin, married December 16, 1912.

11. Quoted in McCool, John H., "Giving Peace a Chance, Sort Of."

12. *San Francisco Chronicle*, January 31, 1917.

13. *San Francisco Examiner*, January 26, 1917, p. 3.

14. Ibid.

15. *San Francisco Examiner*, May 22, 1917, p. 6.

16. Kellogg, John H., *Ladies Guide in Health and Disease. Girlhood, Maidenhood, Wifehood, Motherhood*, Des Moines, Iowa, 1883. quoted in Haller and Haller, p. 135.

17. *San Francisco Examiner*, November 15, 1917, p. 5.

CHAPTER EIGHT

1. Correspondence, Anne Diestal, Archivist, U.S. Federal Bureau of Prisons, to Linda Eversole, August 18, 1998. A thorough search of federal and state records finds no mention of Stella under her various names serving time in any facility, although it was pointed out that some records have been destroyed.

2. Gentry, Curt, *The Madams of San Francisco*. It has been asserted that 337 O'Farrell Street continued as a brothel into the 1930s. Whether this is accurate or not, it is certain Stella was not personally running it.

3. State of California, certificate of Marriage, Estella Bearns and Martin Fabian, November 9, 1920.

4. Correspondence, Mary Rood to Linda Eversole, March 27, 2000.

5. *Times*, August 6, 1923, p. 5.

6. Correspondence, Katherine Lewis to Linda Eversole, July 21, 1993.

7. Record of Funeral—Estella Fabian, April 15, 1946, Jones Mortuary, Lakeport, California.

EPILOGUE

1. Correspondence, Vicki Little, Forest Lawn Memorial Park to Linda Eversole, April 9, 1993.

Sources

PRIMARY AND UNPUBLISHED—CANADA

BC Archives

BC Attorney General—Documents, Correspondence
BC Attorney General—Registers and Indexes to Coroner's Inquiries
    and Inquests
BC Provincial Police Records and Correspondence
BC Supreme Court Orders, Cause Books and Daily Diaries
Census Records—1891, 1901
Central Registry of the Immigration Branch
Divorce Records
Probated Wills
Provincial Commission re: Victoria Police Commissioners—1910
Tax Assessment Rolls—South Saanich, Victoria
Victoria Bills of Sale Indexes and Registers, 1861–1956
Victoria Gaol—Prisoner's Charge and Sentence Book
Victoria Provincial Court Records
Victoria Speedy Trials 1888–1916
Vital Statistics Records—Births, Marriages, Deaths
Wills Index

Saanich Municipal Archives

Clerk's Files—Fire Department Report, 1923
Municipal Clerk's Letter Books, 1907–11
Fire Insurance Plan—1931

City of Victoria Archives

City of Victoria Assessment Rolls—1892–1915
City Bylaws
City Council Minutes
Fire Insurance Plans
Mayors' Reports
Minutes of the Board of Police Commissioners, 1893–1921
Police Court Series—Magistrates Records Books, Charge Books
Subject Files—Hotels and Saloons, Prostitution
Tax Sale Records

Victoria Land Titles Office

Absolute Fee Books, Indefeasible Fee Books, Charge Books,
    Documents Deposited—1899–1920

Victoria Police Archives
> Charge Books—1899–1918
> Mug Shot Books #1, #2 1904–09
> Bulletins 1907, 1910

PRIMARY AND UNPUBLISHED—UNITED STATES

Albuquerque Public Library
> City and Telephone Directories 1898–1920

Alameda, California
> County Recorder, California, Certificate of Death—Martin Fabian, May 20, 1932
> Alameda Free Library—City Directories and Telephone Books

Arizona State Archives
> Divorce Record—Estella H. Curtis vs. Dudley W. Curtis, July 14, 1896, District Court, County of Navajo, Territory of Arizona
> Court Record—Territory of Arizona vs. D. W. Curtis, Assault to Murder, 1896
> Marriage License and Certificate—Jackson F. Durlin and Estella H. Curtis, 1897
> General Index to Deed—Grantors and Grantees 1895–97
> Warranty Deed—Estella Durlin to Minnie Carroll, 1899

California State Library (Sacramento)
> California Death Index
> Voters' Lists

Lakeport, California
> Lake County Recorder's Office—death registration Estella H. Fabian
> Jones Mortuary—Record of Funeral—Estella H. Fabian

San Francisco, California
> Library—Directories and telephone books 1890–1920
> Recorder's Office

State of California
> Department of Health, Bureau of Vital Statistics—Certificate of Marriage—Martin Fabian and Estella H. Bearns, November 9, 1920
> Department of Corrections, Sacramento

State of Missouri
> Department of Health, Bureau of Vital Statistics
> Historical Society (Columbus)

State of Ohio

Bureau of Vital Statistics—Certificate of Death—Curtis, Dudley W.,
March 20, 1914

INTERVIEWS AND CORRESPONDENCE

Carroll, John
Carroll, Roy Harry
Carroll, Dorothy
Dunn, Emma Comfort
Johnson, Byron
Lewis, Katherine
Presson, Dorothy (Crawford County Historical Society)
Rood, Mary
Temple, Cecil

NEWSPAPERS

Lake County Bee (Lakeport, California)
Los Angeles Times
San Francisco Examiner
The People's Press (Victoria, British Columbia)
The Week (Victoria, British Columbia)
Vancouver Province
Vancouver Sun
Victoria Daily Colonist
Victoria Times
Winslow Mail (Winslow, Arizona)

ONLINE RESOURCES

Brigham Young University, Special Collections, Western States Historical
Marriage Record Index
California Death Index
Church of Jesus Christ of Latter Day Saints—Family Search
Ellis Island—Passenger Lists
National Archives of Canada
Ohio Historical Society—Death Index
Rootsweb
San Francisco City Museum
University of Kansas
U.S. Social Security Index

PRIVATE COLLECTIONS

Rood, Mary
Carroll, John
Johnson, Byron

PUBLISHED

Adler, Polly. *A House Is Not A Home*. New York: Rinehart & Co., 1953.

Asbury, Herbert. *The Barbary Coast*. New York: Alfred A Knopf, 1933.

Backhouse, Frances. *Women of the Klondike*. Toronto: Whitecap Books, 1995.

Barnhardt, Jacqueline. *The Fair But Frail: Prostitution in San Francisco, 1840–1900*.
Reno: University of Nevada Press, 1986.

Beck, Warren A. and Ynez D. Haase. *Historical Atlas of New Mexico*. Norman:
University of Oklahoma Press, 1969.

Bell, Ernest A. *Fighting the Traffic in Young Girls or War on the White Slave Trade*.
G. S. Ball, 1910.

Bell, Ernest A. *War on the White Slave Trade*. Toronto: Coles Publishing Co., 1980
(reprint of the 1910 edition that included additional chapters on Canada).

Blanchard, Leola Howard. *Conquest of Southwest Kansas*. Kansas: Wichita
Eagle Press, 1931.

Butler, Anne M. *Daughters of Joy, Sisters of Misery*. Chicago: University of
Illinois Press, 1985.

Clapin, Sylva. *A New Dictionary of Americanisms*. New York: Louis Weiss & Co., 1968
(reprint of 1902 edition).

Crandon. *Surgical After-Treatment: A Manual of the Conduct of Surgical Convalescence*.
Philadelphia: W. B. Saunders Co., 1912.

Dary, David. *Seeking Pleasure in the Old West*. Lawrence, KS: University Press
of Kansas, 1995.

Dunn, Emma J. *Bourbon, Missouri: A Picture History of a Small Town*. (self-published) 1988.

Elliott, Eugene Clinton. *History of Variety—Vaudeville in Seattle*. Seattle: University of
Washington Press, 1944.

Evans, Max. *Madam Millie*. Albuquerque, NM: University of New Mexico Press, 2002.

Gentry, Curt. *The Madams of San Francisco*. Garden City, NY: Doubleday & Co., 1964.

Gerlach, Russell, Dennis Hrebec and Milton Rafferty. *Atlas of Missouri*.
Springfield: Aux-Arc Research Associates, 1970.

Gibson, Arnell Morgan. *Oklahoma: A History of Five Centuries*. Norman:
University of Oklahoma Press, 1981.

Gilfoyle, Timothy J. *City of Eros: New York City, Prostitution, and the Commercialization of Sex,
1790–1920*. New York: W. W. Norton & Company, 1992.

Gray, James. *Red Lights on the Prairies*. Toronto: Macmillan, 1971.

Green, Valerie. *No Ordinary People—The Story of Victoria's Mayors Since 1862*. Victoria, BC: Beach Holme Publishing, 1992.

Haigh, Jane G. and Claire Rudolf Murphy. *Gold Rush Women*. Anchorage, AK: Alaska Northwest Books, 1997.

Hansen-Brett, Lacey. "Ladies in Scarlet: An Historical Overview of Prostitution in Victoria, British Columbia, 1870–1939." Essay, 1984.

Haller, John S. and Robin M. *The Physician and Sexuality in Victorian America*. New York: W. W. Norton & Co., 1974.

Hudson's Bay Company Catalogue—Autumn/Winter 1910–11 (reprint). Winnipeg, MB: Watson & Dwyer Publishing Co., 1977.

Johnson, Byron A. and Sharon P. *Guilded Palaces of Shame—Albuquerque's Redlight Districts 1880–1914*. Albuquerque, NM: Gilded Age Press, 1983.

Keen, William Williams, ed. *Surgery—Its Principles and Practice*, Vol. VIII. Philadelphia: W. B. Saunders Co., 1921.

Kimball, Nell. *Her Life As An American Madam*. New York: Macmillan, 1970.

Latham, Barbara and Cathy Kess, eds. *In Her Own Right—Selected Essays on Women's History*. Victoria: Camosun College, 1980.

Martin's Annual Criminal Code (Police Edition). 2000.

McCool, John H. "Giving Peace a Chance, Sort Of," This Week in KU History (www.kuhistory.com), ed. Henry J. Fortunato, October 2, 2002. University of Kansas Memorial Corporation. (Retrieved November 16, 2004.)

McReynolds, Edwin C. *Oklahoma: A History of the Sooner State*. Norman: University of Oklahoma Press, 1964.

Meier, Gary and Gloria. *Those Naughty Ladies of the Old Northwest*. Bend, OR: Maverick Distributers, 1990.

Minaker, Dennis. *The Gorge of Summers Gone—A History of Victoria's Inland Waterway*. Victoria: Desktop Publishing Ltd., 1998.

Miner, Craig. *West of Wichita: Settling the High Plains of Kansas, 1865–90*. Lawrence, KS: University Press of Kansas, 1986.

Missouri State Gazeteer and Business Directory, 1876–77. St. Louis: R. L. Polk & Co., 1876.

Morgan, Lael. *Good Time Girls of the Alaska-Yukon Gold Rush*. New York: Whitecap Books, 1998.

Moynahan, Jay. *Talkin' About Sportin' Women*. Spokane, WA: Chickadee Publishing, 2002.

Parker, Dave. *First Water, Tigers!* Victoria: Sono Nis Press, 1987.

Pels-Leusden, Friedrich (Gardner, Faxton E., trans.). *Surgical Operations— A Handbook for Students and Practitioners*. New York: Rebman Company, 1912.

Reksten, Terry. *More English Than the English*. Victoria: Orca Book Publishers, 1986.

Roberts, Nickie. *Whores in History: Prostitution in Western Society*. London: Grafton, 1993.

Rosen, Ruth, *The Lost Sisterhood*. Baltimore, MD: University of Johns Hopkins Press, 1982.

Rudgley, Richard. *Essential Substances: A Cultural History of Intoxicants in Society*. New York: Kodansha International, 1993.

Ruede, Howard. *Sod House Days: Letters from a Homesteader, 1877–78*. New York: Cooper Square Publishing Company Inc., 1966.

Ryley, Bay. *Gold Diggers of the Klondike*. Winnipeg, MB: Watson & Dwyer, 1997.

Sauer, Carl O. *Geography of the Ozark Highland of Missouri*. New York: Greenwood Press, 1968.

Self, Huber and Homer E. Socolofsky, *Historical Atlas of Kansas* (2nd ed.). Norman: University of Oklahoma Press, 1988.

Shirk, George H. *Oklahoma Place Names*. Norman: University of Oklahoma Press, 1965.

Smith, Curtis F. *The Brothels of Bellingham*. Bellingham, WA: Whatcom County Historical Society, 2004.

Tannahill, Reay. *Sex in History*. New York: Stein and Day, 1980.

Tefertiller, Casey. *Wyatt Earp: The Life Behind the Legend*. New York: John Wiley and Sons, 1997.

Turner, George H. *Before the Council; or Social Life in Victoria*. Victoria: Department of Agriculture, February 1891.

Weil, Dr. Andrew and Winnifred Rosen. *From Chocolate to Morphine*. Boston: Houghton Mifflin, 1993.

Wells, Evelyn. *Champagne Days of San Francisco*. New York: Doubleday & Co., 1947.

Wolsey, Serge. *Call House Madam*. San Francisco: Martin Tudordale Corp., 1942.

Index